Bernice Kie[illegible]

Plain
REDEMPTION

Amos Raber Jr.

Cover design by: Fonda Martin

Edited by: Kimberly Shumate - Barbara Gordon - Shawn Smucker

Printed in the United States of America
10 9 8 7 6 5 4 3 2 1

This book so beautifully illustrates the covenant of redemption. Just when it seems the roots of a godly heritage are vain, Jesus hears the heart cry of a sin-sick soul. Our Savior then takes the *mess* of sin, applies His precious blood through the *miracle* of redemption and resurrects the reality of Amos's childhood dream. A *message* of hope and inspiration for readers of all ages and stages of life.

-Nelson and Sarah Coblentz,
Executive Director of Gospel Express Ministries

This is a book that will at tug at your heartstrings. A story of how the Lord works and turns tragedy into redemption!

-Eduard & Christine Klassen

Amos Raber's journey through tragedy and pain is a story you will not want to miss. He speaks from the heart of his childhood, his love for music, and his struggles with God in the face of suffering. He bears testimony of the great grace which God gives a broken man or woman

Jerry Eicher,
Author of My Amish Childhood

What an excellent, inspiring read! Addiction, abuse, and the loss of loved ones leaves Amos trying to hold on to life! By the grace of God Amos chooses faith over fear, and love over bitterness. This story is a beautiful picture of what God can do if we allow Him to shine through us in-spite of our circumstances! A highly recommended read!

Linda Miller
Faith View Books

TABLE OF CONTENTS

DEDICATION

This book is dedicated to my wife and children for their uncommon patience and belief in me.

Thank you for your love and support.

The stories and memories in this book are true to my best recollection. To protect the privacy of some people mentioned, a few names, places, and details have been changed without altering the integrity of the event's meaning.

If there are any inaccuracies or misunderstandings in these stories, they are the author's alone. After discussion and if necessary, the author will accept requests for corrections for the next printing.

ACKNOWLEDGMENTS

I am ever grateful for the opportunity to write my story, or at least part of it. I am forever indebted to my Heavenly Father for His saving and sustaining grace in my life and without His Redemption, the story wouldn't be worth telling.

Margaret. Thank you for being my wife, you have been a bigger part of God's redemption in my life than you could ever imagine. Thank you for encouraging me to write my story and for helping to make the time to write in the midst of our busy schedule. I love you so much and I'm truly grateful for the privilege of doing life with you.

To our five children...

Cole, Logan, Brooklyn, Joshua and Brielle

I love you with all my heart and thank God for the privilege of walking beside you as you grow. I never knew I could love so deeply, and I will forever treasure in my heart all the memories and smiles you give me. My prayer is that you will always maintain a soft heart toward your heavenly Father and His perfect will for your life. Therein is the only place of true peace and contentment.

I bless you, as your earthly father, with the words of our Heavenly Father,

"These are my beloved children, in whom I am well pleased!'

I would also like to thank everyone that helped me recall memories including my parents, Amanda's family, several of Amanda's friends and lots of my friends and relatives. People have encouraged me over the years to write a book, but I was never willing to take the time to go for a walk down memory lane. Now, I am so glad I did. Over the past one and half years of writing, I've responded in multiple ways.

Sometimes I was overwhelmed with warmth as I recalled precious moments from my childhood, other times I felt a chill in my spine when recalling something not so pleasant. I also laughed a lot. My family would come running to see what I was laughing about. Normally I would stop writing and share the story with them. I also wept. Sometimes memory lane seemed as dark and lonely as it did the day it happened. My chest burned with pain just like it did in that particular moment many years ago. Sometimes I wept freely as the tears flowed down my cheeks. They weren't always tears of sadness, sometimes they were tears of solemn joy as I marveled at God's sovereignty.

HOME SWEET HOME

At five in the morning our house came alive
We were up and ready to meet the day
Milking cows by hand I couldn't understand
Why life had to be that way

It was Mama's good cooking and Daddy's hard whupping
That kept us on the straight and narrow way
We went church on Sunday, back to work on Monday
It was the only life this country boy had known
And it's stamped on my heart as home sweet home

BBQ burgers fresh off the grill
Mama sure knew how to do them well
Sitting on the front porch eating homemade ice cream
Now seems like a dream

There's a special place in my heart for that eighty-acre farm
Sitting up on a hill off the old dirt road
Where this little barefoot country boy thought he was a slave
Sometimes he'd do anything to go back to those days

—Amos Raber Jr.

Chapter One

HELP! WE NEED HELP!

It was actually official: Amanda and I were married. The first half of our honeymoon was over, but we still had another week before going back to work. We planned to spend the first few days moving our belongings over to the Waky House, then the rest of the time just tidying up and making it our home.

It was Monday, December 30th, and we started our day around midmorning. We needed to go into Goshen for some supplies. I went out and started the car so my bride would have a warm ride into town.

"Hey, Sweets," I said as I came back into the apartment, "we're still on our honeymoon. After we pack, let's go and I'll treat you to a meal at Ponderosa."

"Sounds good," she replied with a smile.

We made the short drive into Goshen and within a few minutes, were seated at a table for two. Although our chit-chat flowed freely, we couldn't afford to lose track of time. It was moving day and we had lots to do!

Back at the apartment, we got busy packing her things: small bags, big bags, boxes of all sizes, all holding something valuable to her. We started carrying things out of the apartment and stacking them neatly in the back of the Ford SUV. Finally, it was full. The rest of her items and mine in Millersburg would have to be taken to our new house in another load.

"Mr. Raber," she said with a sheepish grin, "Don't you think you should let me drive? It is my SUV ya know."

We had recently traded her car in for the larger vehicle, and she was excited to drive it. There was some snow on the ground along with heavy fog hovering in the air, but the temperature had risen a bit. Driving was a little dangerous because of the patchy mist, worse in some places than others.

With a wink, I took a seat behind the wheel instead.

We turned left onto US Highway 6 and headed west on the way to our new home.

"Hey, Sweets," I said, "I'm going to take a slight detour and show you where my new boss lives."

As we traveled through the soupy air, we got lost in conversation and, being new to the area, I wasn't familiar with the roads.

Suddenly, the road I was looking for was upon us. As I attempted to slow down for the turn, I found an 18-wheeler in my rearview mirror bearing down on us. I couldn't risk an accident, so I chose the next road and we would just have to backtrack a little.

We safely slowed and turned onto Elkhart County Road 9 heading north. The local country radio station was playing a new song by Patty Loveless called "How Can I Help You to Say Goodbye." It was one of our favorites, and we sang along, not really paying that much attention to the meaning of it. And the fog persisted as I drove slowly, holding hands with Amanda across the center console.

It was a moment that I never wanted to end.

Just the two of us enjoying life together; just a couple of honeymooners in love.

Without warning, Amanda sat forward and screamed, "Stop sign!" but it was too late.

We were already entering the intersection when an oncoming pickup truck crashed into Amanda's side of the SUV. We spun in circles and came to rest in the field across the road.

I was knocked unconscious. When I woke up, my head hurt and my knee ached. I looked over and saw my new bride as she sat there with her hands in her lap, her head limp against the back of the seat.

What just happened? I thought. *What is that noise?*

I tried to open the door to get around the car as quickly as I could, but pain raced through my leg. I managed to get out and look in the direction of the noise. My brain was as foggy as the atmosphere.

Finally, I could see—people standing in a neighbor's yard across the road. *What are they doing?* I thought. But it didn't matter. I needed to help Amanda.

The door was dented, but I managed to pry it open.

"Amanda," I called weakly, but she didn't move as if she were sleeping. There was no sign of injury, not at first. But then I saw a gash and some blood on the side of her head just behind her eye, I grabbed her arm and shook her harder.

"Amanda!" I called. She still didn't move.

Panic gripped me and a tsunami of fear overwhelmed my senses. I tried one more time, but to no avail. Turning around, I fell to my knees and hit the dirt, crying out, "Oh God, please don't let her die!"

As the bleak outline of the sun tried to break through the low-lying clouds, I thought for a moment that perhaps God was punishing me for things I had done in my past. I begged God to forgive me, and there on my knees in that field, I committed to follow God for the rest of my life no matter what.

Exhausted and still muddled, I started walking as fast as I could towards the people across the road.

"We need help!" I yelled. "We need help!"

Then I heard sirens in the distance.

Reeling with shock and exhaustion, I buried my head in my hands and wept. How was it possible that our world could change so drastically in mere seconds? Would this be the end to more than our honeymoon?

Chapter Two

HELLO LIFE!

It was a fair, sunny February day in Daviess County, Indiana. In many ways, I'm sure it was typical in that little Old Order Amish community, with the regular hustle and bustle of life going on. After the routine chores were all done, the three Raber children left with the pony and cart for the two-mile drive to the local Amish school.

Since it was a Monday, Dad would normally have been gone already. But on this day, he stayed home to care for his wife. Her labor had started during the night—her fifth pregnancy—and that dawn broke with new hope and expectancy.

The fact that Dad was even home undoubtedly created some curiosity among the older siblings as they left for school. Mom had no doubt been busy preparing the house for her absence with cleaning, baking, and mending clothes.

She did the laundry and hung it out on the wash line to dry behind the house. Dad did some work around the farm, perhaps mucking out the stalls or mending a fence that a horse had kicked over. I wasn't there, not yet, but I write this based on our growing up days as well as Mom's recollections.

It was 4:00pm when Dad rushed to the neighbors to use the phone to call the taxi driver known in the community as "Doc Hill." After finishing the chores, he hurried the other four children off to Uncle Joe's house across the field then flew into the house to get dressed. When Doc arrived, Mom and Dad folded themselves into his shabby old car and raced off to the hospital in the nearby town.

Doctor Fraiser was our family physician, and immediately began caring for Mom. One hour later, it was official.

"It's a boy!" Doctor Fraiser announced.

On Monday, February 17th, at 6:30pm, I was born weighing in at seven pounds, one ounce.

Mom and Dad had the name chosen ever since they knew Mom was with child. If it was a girl, she would be Lydia, named after my Mom's mother. And if it was a boy, they would pass on the namesake of my father, Amos H. Raber.

A few days later, the three of us arrived back on our 80-acre farm to begin my life in Montgomery, Indiana. Mom, Dad, and me...

... Amos Raber Jr.

My parents now had five children: Marlin Ray, 10; Kenneth Lee, 9; Regina Rose, 6; Olen Jay, 4; and me.

†††

As far as I was concerned, there was no greater place in all the world than Montgomery, Indiana. Our house sat up on a little knob off a back road with very little traffic. When someone did go by, we normally recognized the vehicle. Our property consisted of our house, a barn, the grinding shed, a tool shop and milk house, the chicken house, the turkey barn, and a pig building we called the feeding floor.

One of my very first memories was when I was three years old. My parents decided to put a short brick wall around the front of the house. My dad was, and remains, a hard worker. It was a hot, sultry day in southern Indiana, and Dad was getting the bricks cut to size and placing them. He was using an old-fashioned barrel mixer with a little engine attached to mix up the mortar. I watched carefully as he walked back and forth, carting those heavy buckets of concrete. He would start the job after the morning chores then keep at it throughout the day, stopping only for lunch and maybe a few cold drink breaks.

We always had at least a dozen or so of the tall, sixteen-ounce glass bottles in the milk house. They stayed ice cold in the water tank where the milk cans were cooled after each milking and prepared for the milkman to pick up the next day. I was ever-fascinated by my dad's ability to get the job done. He had what seemed like an endless stream of energy and strength, but I'm sure he tired more often than I could see.

I admired him so much!

What was my role? I played with leftover pieces of bricks Dad had cut, and occupied myself quite well as I tried to build something of my own. You could say I had a very healthy imagination.

Meanwhile, my father set bricks until he ran out of mortar, and then it was time to pour a few more bags of dry powder into the mixer, add water, and start the engine. That old Wisconsin four-cycle motor was by no means new and it didn't have a self-winding starting rope. It always needed some additional coaxing before it would run the way it was supposed to, but that wasn't a problem since Dad was a mechanic.

I watched as he leaned over the engine and made some adjustments to the carburetor. I also remember seeing the starter rope dangling from his hand.

Dangling... dangling.

Suddenly, the rope caught in the crankshaft, spinning out of control, and rapidly tightened up. It slipped off his hand.

But not his little finger.

The next thing I saw was Dad jumping around, hunched over and clutching his hand as he moaned in pain. Adrenaline raced through me as I stood helplessly watching. A few hours later—due to some old-time story about faster and better healing—Dad's little finger got a proper burial just on the other side the lawn fence.

May it still rest in peace.

Chapter Three

IN THE HANDS OF MY FATHER

Eighty acres doesn't sound that big now, but as a young boy it seemed like half the universe.

A farm like ours held highlights for every season of the year, but spring was extra special. After a cold dreary winter, spring brought new life in every way imaginable.

The animals seemed to anticipate the change as much as we did. They had spent those last several frosty months eating hay and stored grain, but soon the pastures turned green and they enjoyed the fresh, luscious grass. The brown lawn developed a sage tint, and soon enough we'd get the push mowers out of the shop and take them to Dad. Then he performed his annual maintenance and sharpening of the blades before starting the mowing season.

After a few long pulls on the starter rope, the little Honda engine coughed out some white smoke and roared to life. Oh, the excitement of that first mowing as we pushed that cranky cohort across the lawn as it chewed up and spit out all it could eat.

In those days, sleep seemed like an absolute waste of time, and morning couldn't come soon enough. My eyes opened as I awoke to the sound of birds chirping and Dad working outside. I'd hear him singing through the open window as I got ready, so I knew he was close by. Maybe he was mixing a batch of feed for the animals or getting the horses harnessed and hitched to the plow for a day of turning the sod, preparing it for seeding.

It took me mere seconds to jump out of bed, get dressed, and barely stop to say "hi" to Mom as I ran through the kitchen on my race outside to find Dad.

One morning, I sprinted to the barnyard where he had two horses hitched to the manure spreader. With one scoop at a time, he would load the spreader. And when he looked up and saw me hanging on the side of the gate, he stopped for a break and walked over to me.

With one hand on the gate and the other resting on the shovel, he stood there smiling, sweat dripping off his nose.

"Good morning, Son," he said cheerfully as he repeated his favorite sunrise dictum. "If every morning would be as nice as this morning, it would be a nice morning every morning. Why don't you run up to the milk house and grab a cold bottle of soda for me?"

It didn't take me long, especially since I was sure he would share some of it with me. I raced to the milk house and stuck my hand in the frigid water where the milk cans from that morning's milking cooled in preparation for the milk man. Finding one frosty bottle of suds, I gripped it tightly and dashed back to the barnyard gate where Dad waited. He'd reach for the bottle with one hand and into his pocket with the other, pulling out his pliers. With one quick motion, the sealed cap was gone.

Without any hesitation, he put the beverage to his lips and raised the bottom high into the air. I watched in awe as Dad's Adam's Apple bobbed in rhythm to the once-full container that was suddenly nearly empty. At some point, he paused for a breath.

"Wow, that's good!" he exclaimed.

Then, he'd hand it to me for a few swallows, but only a few since the temperature of the liquid was hard on my throat. He'd then lovingly tell me to return the empty bottle back to the milk house for recycling.

It felt like his hands could do anything.

MY DAD

I'd get up in the morning, wipe the sleep from my eyes
I'd look out through the window at the early sunrise
That's when I'd hear his voice, across the air waves
It's a part of my memory that will never, never fade
He was a hard-working man from his head down to his toes
I loved to watch him work as the sweat dripped from his nose
He'd lean upon his shovel with a hearty "Good Morning,
If they'd all be this way it'd be a nice morning every morning!"

Chorus
And he'd sing "What a beautiful day for my Lord to come again
What a beautiful day for Him to take His children home"
I loved to watch him sing, he'd give it all he had
And I remind myself of him, he's the man I call my dad

He was good with a hammer, a chisel and a plow
No matter how it looked he could fix it somehow
He'd mend all the fences with a smile upon his face

There's not another man that could ever take his place
He chose to raise a family, some little girls and boys
And when he went to pick a wife he made the perfect choice
He never started something that he could not get done
That precious little woman is the one I call my mom

And he'd sing "What a beautiful day for my Lord to come again
What a beautiful day for Him to take His children home"
I loved to watch him sing, he'd give it all he had
And I remind myself of him, he's the man I call my dad

—Amos Raber Jr.

I must have been around five years old when a few big trucks with massive drills pulled into our driveway. After they spoke with Dad for several minutes, the men in the trucks made their way out into the field where they started the drilling process, testing our land for veins of coal.

Sure enough, they found it!

The day finally arrived when you could see them coming from a distance—a convoy of big, yellow, heavy equipment leaving a cloud of dust as they rumbled across the gravel roads of Daviess County.

They were strip mining our property, and I was overly fascinated by the sight. I sat for hours and watched as the huge Drag Line bucket thundered to the ground, pulled forward by a huge cable—the bucket forced into the ground by its own weight. As the cable hoisted the overflowing bucket into the air, the driver rotated the machine to dump the earth onto the growing pile. The big diesel engine puffed clouds of black smoke as it struggled under the weight.

The bull dozers were slow but mighty as they chugged back and forth; the driver raising and lowering the massive blade. I could hardly take it all in. The Coal Bowl Scrapers were similar to a tractor trailer combination. As they drove, they dropped the center of their machine, which appeared to be a big basin. As the bowl scraped the ground, the dirt would begin to fill the container.

It was amazing since they had the ability to create their own train. If the ground was especially hard or if it was muddy, each Bowl Scraper was equipped with a hook in the front and a heavy pin in the rear. They would simply hook on to each other and create a team, pulling all together in one accord.

They worked a long time to strip off the dirt. And what seemed to be without warning appeared a gigantic hole in the middle of our field. It was a huge pit when they had finally reached the coal and were ready for the trucks to haul it out.

The dump trucks and semi-trucks came and went in an endless parade, meeting each other as they shared our little gravel roads. They drove down into the pit and waited for their turn to be filled, the loader giving the maximum amount. Then, the horn would sound!

When the waiting driver heard the blast of noise, he immediately started the intense trek up the steep hill as the machine shuttered under the load, diesel engine belching black smoke.

One by one, they came and went.

We were strictly forbidden to play on the machinery, but in the evening when the cows were all milked and the mining workers had left, those big yellow machines were a welcoming sight. My siblings and I would sneak across the field and play on them as long as we could, until we heard the faint sound of Mom or Dad calling for us.

My favorite part of the coal mine was a dozer driver who went by the name of Randy Chicken Man. He was such a cheerful kind guy! With Mom's permission, my siblings and I would go and stand at a safe distance while we watched the miners, and when Randy Chicken Man would see us coming across the field, he would wave and sound his horn. I think he loved the attention as much as we did.

During his break, he would bring his loud clanging dozer to a stop close by the fence where we stood. Even before he opened his door we could hear his laughter. Then the moment we waited for...

...he'd invite us into his dozer and offer each one of us a lollipop.

It's funny what you remember as a kid. Mounds of dirt, cold drinks and lollipops, and the hands of men that seemed so invincible.

Like the hands of my father.

Like my hands before the accident.

Now, I was standing in another field...

...my hands helpless as my new wife Amanda lay unconscious in the front seat.

Chapter Four

LIFE ON THE FARM

After the coal mine went through, it left us with two ponds that became my hangout when I wasn't working the farm. Catfish, bass, and bluegill were the daily catch.

One afternoon while fishing, I found a crippled Mallard duckling. I quickly rescued it and took it to the old chicken house that wasn't being used. I found a heater hood the perfect size. I filled it with water from the pond, hoping to make the duckling feel right at home, but I wasn't convinced it did.

I loved the little duck's company, and marveled at its elegant feathers. But no matter how much I tried, that little duckling never seemed to develop mutual feelings. Finally, I heeded Dad's advice and carried the bird to the pond, releasing it back into the wild.

I loved spending time at our two ponds fishing or swimming. But fishing always required bait, which meant I needed to find a shovel and a spot where I thought there might be earth worms. But in the spring, that task was easier. All I needed to do was go out to the field where Dad was plowing with a team of horses and a single bottom plow. I could quickly fill my empty pork-and-beans container with worms as I trailed behind him and pulled them from the freshly turned sod.

Then off to the pond I went.

Other times, I would get one of my brothers to go to the woods and explore with me, maybe even build a tepee.

I also spent a lot of time at the sandbox. There on my knees playing with my toy semi, the world seemed within my grasp, and my imagination ran wild. In my mind, I drove halfway around creation.

Growing up on a farm had its own ways of charming a young lad. I remember walking to the far corner of the acreage with my older sister Regina and our dog Shep, kicking up the dust with our bare feet as we went to fetch the cows for milking time. Milking time was whatever we made it, filled with the normal sibling fussing and arguments or other times, the little milking parlor rang with laughter as we showed off, told stories from school, or passed on the latest gossip.

There was always lots of hard work to be done on an Amish farm, especially since our church wasn't allowed to have skid loaders. It meant that our hands were accustomed to a scoop shovel at a very early age.

One of our jobs included grinding and mixing feed for the animals. Sometimes that meant climbing into a dusty bin filled with oats or shoveling ear corn from an outside corn crib. Either way, it was a hard, loud job. The John Deere tractor roared as it turned the shaft that powered the Arts-Way grinder mixer.

We stayed busy shoveling the ear corn into the hopper until at last the grinder bin was full. There was a feeling of satisfaction and accomplishment when the boisterous tractor was slowed to an idle and the mixer wound down to a stop. After a moment of rest and a cold drink, the ringing in our ears would subside as we would move on to the barnyard where the hungry cows were eagerly awaiting the feast we had just prepared.

†††

Dad worked for my uncle Roman in the horse collar manufacturing business. The shop was approximately four miles from our house, and since Dad enjoyed racehorses, he often had a horse he was training. The exciting part about driving the horse cart to work was that his cart was similar to those used in actual racing. It was very lightweight, had one seat, and didn't have a floor to rest your feet on.

Dad sat on the seat with me beside him on the frame. It was thrilling—the sparse seating and no floor was an adventure. But the highest excitement came when Dad clucked and signaled the young racehorse to take the speed up a notch or two. Oh, the freedom of watching the road speed by right under us while we raced down the road behind that magnificent animal!

In those days, the Daviess County Amish church districts were not allowed to use "Top Buggies"—buggies with roofs to shield riders from the rain or cold. They were normally constructed of light wood framing then wrapped in vinyl or painted. However, families with young children had what we called a "rumble"—a little vinyl cover over the back of the buggy that sheltered the seats where the children rode.

Riding in that little rumble holds some of my earliest memories of family singing. We were riding home from Grandpa Yoder's house (my mother's parents) on a cool, dark autumn evening. The physical comfort of being in the rumble was not to be outmatched by the deep satisfaction of hearing my parents and siblings singing together.

How I wish I could remember the song.

Top buggies were used in many other communities, but not in ours. Yet, as many had predicted, progress was inevitable. Sure enough, after some people got them anyway, and others continually suggested that it was time to move into the future, and the change finally came. This was a big deal, especially to the young folks since this would add real class to their Rumspringa. Ben E. Wagler was the officiating bishop that ushered in the new convenience, and as a young, red-blooded boy, I was particularly grateful.

†††

As we worked hard throughout the year, we never lost sight of how special our community was. And just our way of life—living on a farm together.

Our milking parlor, located on the north end of the barn could hold five cows at a time. The number of cows we milked fluctuated with the time of year, and how many cows had given birth to baby calves. Sometimes as few as three and others times up to fourteen!

Oh, the baby calves. It was quite exhilarating to wake up in the morning and hear Dad announce that another cow had a baby during the night. Often, he would stay awake into the wee hours keeping watch for the health of the mama cow during her labor, and the new born calf was my responsibility! Teaching a baby calf to drink from a bottle could be entertaining as it wobbled and struggled to keep its balance, almost like it was on stilts.

As a general rule, we started the milking around 5:00am, then again at 4:30pm. My sister Regina was kind enough to let me milk my favorite cow, Blackie. Meanwhile, she tackled the hardest one.

The infamous Jane!

Milking cows by hand came with its own charms and heartaches.

My brother Olen found great joy in pointing the teat toward his mouth and drinking the warm milk.

"It can't get any fresher than this," he'd say with a sheepish grin.

The worst terror that any cow could bring the vulnerable milker was to start kicking its hind legs. I recall the sickening feeling of watching all the milk I had coerced with so much verve start rolling down the manure trough, which rendered the morning a complete waste.

The only thing worse that could happen was to have Dad walk in and see the spilled milk. It was a great loss to him since spilled milk was mislaid income and he needed it to clothe and feed his family.

My dad was convinced that hard work never killed anyone, but I wasn't so sure, and certainly not willing to take any risks.

There's something about the weather in the valley of southern Indiana in July that has a way of dragging a body down. Without fail, just when we had 800 bales of hay that needed to be put into the barn, it would turn out to be the hottest day of the year. We would tell our uncles and cousins that we were going to have hay ready to start loading at a certain time, and they would always come and help, no matter how hot it got.

And the saying, "Many hands make light work" rings true.

We had multiple crews throwing the bales on, wagon after wagon. The higher the stack got, the more the young men could show off their strength. The wagon creaked and groaned under the weight as the team of horses pulled it toward the barn. Yes, it was hot out in the field, but that couldn't be compared to the sweltering heat of the haymow as we neatly stacked the hundreds of bails.

It seemed like it couldn't be too soon before Mama brought a nice treat for the toasty, tired crew. My favorite was egg sandwiches along with ice cold chocolate milk.

One would think that as exhausted as everyone was, it would be a time of quiet and rest. But that certainly wasn't the case, and notably if Uncle Fred was around. He seemed to have an endless line of dry comments that would have the rest of us laughing in a matter of seconds.

Life on the farm!

While hard work was as common as the air we breathed, it was also accompanied by the richness of our heritage.

Somehow, stories from our family's past always seemed to find their way into our discussions. Like where and how music became such an important part of the Raber family's life. I loved it when Dad and some of his brothers got that distant look in their eyes as they began recalling the memories. As the music history unfolded, we realized it had all started with my dad's older brother, Uncle David.

Little did I know how much he would influence the man I would eventually become.

Chapter Five

SONG OF DAVID

As much as I cherished the melodic talent in our family, it only deepened when I understood the history behind it all.

The year was 1961, and the Raber house was filled with excitement. Uncle David and Sylvia had been courting, and now marriage was on the horizon. However, there was one thing that would make their young married days trying: the Vietnam War was raging, and David was called into service.

He appealed as a CO (conscientious objector) and was appointed to serve at a hospital in Terre Haute, Indiana.

The wedding was in October of that year, and just a few weeks later, David and his young bride moved to Terre Haute where he would go on active duty. Over the next few months, a serious pain developed in his leg. After numerous X-rays and eventually a biopsy, the doctor's diagnosis came in.

Uncle David had cancer.

The doctor advised that they amputate his leg immediately, but Sylvia refused to sign the papers. They transferred him to a different hospital to see another doctor, but within a short amount of time, his leg was taken—right above the knee.

When they arrived back home, they were met by caring friends and neighbors who felt more like family. Through his connection in the service, David had made some quality buddies that were in similar service in Indianapolis, and they planned to come visit.

They showed up in strapping alpha male fashion, full of life and energy to spare. They were known as the Iowa Boys. But there was one thing evident in their lives: Their love for their suffering friend, David.

There were some younger siblings around my grandfather's house who were especially infatuated with their zeal and love for life. Spellbound by the rumbling exhaust of the muscle car the boys drove, the siblings realized such an impression paled in comparison to when they heard the visiting boys sing.

Oh, they could croon, and it was contagious!

My uncles, aunts, and my dad couldn't get enough of it. The Iowa Boys blended their voices together, singing in four-part harmony—a sound that my dad and his siblings had rarely heard, but desperately wanted to learn.

A few months later, David's cancer spread to his other leg, and only two years after his diagnosis, my uncle passed away. He left behind his young widow Sylvia and a grieving family. True to their character, on the day of the funeral, the Iowa Boys visited to pay their respects to their friend, his family, and his widow. That evening after the funeral, they gathered to sing. It was like healing balm to hear the Iowa Boys raise their voices in sweet harmony.

"There is sweet rest in Heaven," they sang, as if lifting their assurance to David.

Afterward, the Iowa Boys returned to service and eventually, back to their homes. But the memories were still very much alive for my grandfather's children. The Iowa Boys' legacy planted a seed, a dream in the hearts and minds of their friend's younger siblings that would not easily be squelched.

As sad and exciting as it was, the siblings' newfound love of singing would prove to be a real challenge for Grandpa. It totally consumed five of his fourteen children for months and months. When a task around the farm was assigned, it normally ended up in a singing session. The siblings would secretly gather to practice their vocal parts and techniques instead of doing their chores.

Sunday mornings were the hardest. Getting the children up and out of bed for daily chores, milking the cows, eating breakfast, and then getting to church by 9am was difficult enough when everything went well. But Grandpa wasn't prepared for the problems their singing created in his home.

After the chores were done and everyone finally got to the breakfast table, I'm sure Grandpa thought he was in the homestretch of getting his family off to church on time, but he was wrong.

"Girls, please hurry and help your mother get the dishes washed," he ordered. "Boys, go upstairs and get ready so you're done when the girls get up there."

After prayer, Grandpa went outside to complete some last small chores and get the family horse hitched to the buggy for the drive to church. When he made it back in the house, he expected to find the children following the orders he gave. Instead, he was met with the sound of them caroling. Oh, the girls were washing the dishes alright, but they were accompanied by the boys sitting on the counter.

This zeal for singing wasn't some overnight infatuation. It was a flair that never lost its flame. Even in the midst of getting married and having families of their own, my aunts and uncles always made time for singing together. For as long as I can remember, they have made the rounds in the community to perform for the sick, elderly, and the widowed.

Certain blessings just need to be shared.

†††

As a child, I was the beneficiary of the seed planted so many years before by the Iowa Boys. I always excitedly anticipated the evenings when my parents, aunts, and uncles would go sing and I could tag along.

When we reached our destination for the evening and after a friendly welcome from the residents, my dad, his brothers, sisters, and their spouses all found their places around the family table. It was located centrally so everyone in the house could hear when the music began.

My dad and one of his brothers sang bass while others were on tenor, high tenor, and alto with a blend of male and female voices that in my mind could be matched by no other.

There on Dad's lap, my heart was at rest. Yes, I'm sure there was brokenness of every kind back then, just like there is now. But surrounded by people I knew and trusted, everything was all right.

After an hour or so, the lady of the house normally brought out some snacks, and the fellowship began. Soon enough, the room was filled with the buzz of conversation, and if someone wasn't familiar with the Rabers' routine on such an evening, they may have thought it was all over, but it wasn't.

The best was yet to come!

Two of my uncles would go out to the entrance where their coats or jackets were and grab their Hohner (auto valve) harmonicas. As a whole, the Amish people don't use stringed instruments, therefore the harmonica is the instrument of choice in nearly all Amish communities.

My dad and uncles favored the key of E, and once they were all ready, they'd start the song, each carrying their own part—three harmonicas playing in perfect harmony was such a special treat.

It was at one of these sing-alongs when I first experienced the drawing of the Holy Ghost. The song was "O Why Not Tonight?" I remember an intense urge in my heart.

I want to live for God.

Yes, that's what I wanted to do. I wasn't very old, but certainly old enough to realize that life as a whole was filled with disappointments, and I had heard enough about Heaven to know it was a place I wanted to go.

The hot tears welled up in my eyes as I sat there in the safety of my family, surrounded by the chorus of their love. I was overwhelmed with a sense of peace. Looking back, I'm grateful that singing wasn't confined to a community event, but was alive and active right in my own home.

One of my favorite ways to spend an evening was with music. When I saw Dad sitting idle after supper with his feet kicked up, in my mind it was a perfect opportunity to sing. Off to the bedroom I ran to fetch the harmonica to see if I could persuade him.

I found success most nights.

Dad would play and I sang. I begged him to teach me how to traverse the mouthpiece, but he would always respond with a kind smile.

"I can't teach you what you must learn for yourself."

It made no sense to me. How was I to learn if no one showed me? And for months to come, every time I blew on it, I always ended up frustrated and defeated. But Dad insisted that I just keep trying if I really wanted to play badly enough.

A new harmonica from the local Amish store cost $37 plus taxes. I had no money to buy it, and Dad didn't want to invest that much unless he knew I was committed. So, he made a deal with me.

"I'll give you one of my harmonicas that I don't use anymore, and if you learn how to play one song on it, I'll take you to the store and buy a brand new one just for you."

Hohner auto valve in the key of E was the one he chose to let me practice on. I blew and blew on it and vowed to never quit until I had learned to play it. I practiced while I did my chores, after dinner, and while I laid in bed until I fell asleep.

I grew up listening to a variety of country, bluegrass, and gospel artists, but no one was better than Marlin Wagler from my own community. Our family attended a local business' customer appreciation day where I was surprised and pleased to find Marlin Wagler and his group, the Sunlight Gospel Singers, performing.

I was enamored by the whole scene—real microphones, several instruments, and last but not least, the harmonies. And I took it all in. One of the musicians played a snow white acoustic guitar. The buzz of conversation from those around me didn't hinder me from listening intently. My eyes were locked.

So, what does a little Amish boy do with a big dream? He does the best he can with what he has, and does what any other little boy would do.

He pretends!

The closest thing I could find to a microphone was a corncob. That's right. A cob! No kernels, just the bare stock. I was also surprised at how well a few bales of hay can work for a stage. Don't you just love a child's ability to dream? In my imagination, I sang for thousands.

Eventually, reality set in.

I was still just a little Amish boy supposed to be doing my chores.

Lo and behold, one day I figured out how to play "Where the Soul of Man Never Dies." I was fourteen years old by then, and I played it nonstop for fear that I would suddenly forget how. And, true to his word, my dad took me to the store and bought the promised harmonica.

It was all my own, I had earned it!

It came in a nice, shiny, blue and red cardboard case, and I held it in total amazement. My very first instrument! I was now a musician—perhaps in the smallest sense—but still a musician.

With my entry into music, I was always on the lookout for music in all its forms. Whether riding with a taxi driver and listening to the radio or sitting at a restaurant where there was a TV, I always hoped music would find me.

Years later as I lumbered around the farm doing the routine chores, I suddenly received inspiration to write my very first song. I ran into the house, raced upstairs, found a pen and paper, and was soon sitting at the kitchen table.

I wrote as fast as I possibly could, and when I was done, the title came to me.

"Time."

TIME

Can I have just one minute of your time, dear brother
There is something that I've got, walking through my mind
I know you are busy with so many things to do
But how I need an answer if you can spare the time

Do we take enough time with our children, dear brother
Teaching and praying to ease their troubled mind
Giving them love, the kind of love they need
Can you tell me, dear brother, do we take enough time?

We are all so busy trying to earn an extra dime
The next thing we know our children all are grown
Now our children are grown and we have our extra dime
I wonder, dear brother, did we take enough time

Now all those riches that we earned in this world
Will not make a difference when we get our reward
So, let's love, teach, and pray and keep in our minds
That we would be much happier if we took a little more time

—Amos Raber Jr.

Chapter Six

SOMETHING EXTREME

I could go on about fond memories without mentioning any of the negative things, but that wouldn't be fair. It's hard to appreciate the victory on the mountaintop if you don't understand the battle in the valley. Like the car crash that I was now living through. Standing in that field along the road while still on my honeymoon, I soon heard the squeal of sirens in the distance as my dear Amanda slumped in the front seat of the SUV.

But I wasn't thinking about the many blows that I had experienced up to that point that slowly shaped me into who I had become. But as with all life stories, there are difficult moments that God works out for the good.

† † †

There comes a time in every child's life when we began to shed our innocence and, as a result of living in a fallen world, our fond memories start to get muddled with the uglier things that are out there. We become recipients of the positive things in our culture, but we undoubtedly inherit a part of the negative things, as well. And the negative doesn't always look negative to a boy who is ready and willing to do what it takes to transform into a man—a real man. And my definition of manhood was based on one thing: My role models.

Somewhere in the first ten years of my life, I had access to things like tobacco and alcohol. I still have those bitter memories of the very first times I had the courage to light a cigarette. Lighting it was easy, but inhaling it was a whole different ball game. The chest pains, the coughing and spitting was a natural body response, but I had to conquer it for the adventure to continue.

After all, that's what men do.

There was nothing as cool as watching an adult take a long drag off a smoke as the fire lit up on the end of the cigarette, followed by the misty stream pouring slowly out of their mouth. Sometimes, they would exhale through their mouth and nose at the same time! Amazing!

That was my goal, and I had finally reached it. By adolescence, I was a full-time addicted smoker. Disciplined repeatedly for my misbehavior, my desire was still greater than the fear, and I pressed on.

This was an exciting age to be alive!

I learned about life by watching those around me, and I experienced a lot of things for the first time in those tender years.

When I was around ten years old, I was with a group of peers at an Amish school outing or a Sunday after service adventure—I can't remember which. But I do remember the barn, the hosting peer (I'll call him Isaac), and the moment "it" happened.

We were playing some games in the yard, running, yelling, and laughing like any group of young boys would, when suddenly I noticed we were being called to a team meeting. Isaac was in the center of the huddle talking in hushed tones.

What is going on? I wondered.

I didn't catch it all, but I got enough to realize that there was something unusual he wanted to show us in the barn haymow.

Probably a flock of graceful pigeons or a coon that came up from the woods and decided to have her babies in the warmth of the straw.

Whatever it was, it sure did seem appealing and promising, so I trailed behind the stream of boys as we raced toward the barn. We flew around the corner, through the gate, and into the ground level of the weathered building. One by one, we scrambled up the old single rung ladder and bounced onto the floor of the haymow.

I was toward the tail end of the line, so by the time I set foot onto the old creaking hay-covered wooden floor, everyone else had already gathered in the corner. I couldn't catch a glimpse right away, so I crowded in through the maze of boys.

And there it was.

Pornography.

I had never seen anything like it before, but the moment I saw it there was an instant darkness that hung in the atmosphere of that barn. My heart raced with guilt. Wicked guilt. The innocent fun of our afternoon had suddenly dissolved in a heavy hush. The poorly lit, sultry haymow suddenly felt more like a prison.

In the world of young boys and their peers, everything is a contest. And it was very clear this wasn't the first presentation for Isaac. He was well versed in this book. He eagerly flipped from one page to another pointing out details that he considered the most intriguing.

No shame at all.

Though his audience rapidly dwindled, Isaac never faltered. He stood tall and proud as the supplier of something so extreme. This was not a fish story that was hard to believe, or a monstrous buck he claimed to have seen in the woods.

This... this was something entirely alien.

Some of the boys were chuckling while others made comments, uttering words of disapproval.

After several minutes of gazing, our little group dispersed and scurried back down the old rickety wooden ladder and out into the lawn for more games. It was almost like it never happened. And as far as the rest of the world was concerned, it hadn't.

But it had.

I don't remember the month, what we ate for lunch, or what brought the group of boys together. But I do remember the barn, the book, and the knot in my stomach.

The ride home that afternoon was agonizing. The clip-clop of the horse's hooves and the crunching gravel that normally serenaded me sounded distant and hollow.

Everything within me screamed that it was all damnable, but what was even more tormenting was that there was a small part of me that wanted to see more. And would I ever be able to rid myself of that vile memory.

† † †

My brothers and neighbor boys were avid coon hunters, and as I got older, I jumped at every chance to trail along. For me, nothing was as fun as that hobby. I loved the adventurous part of going out at night and listening to the jokes and stories from the older boys. The only part I hated was walking what seemed like miles to follow the hounds.

Sometimes they found a nearby wandering coon and would run it up a tree, and our hunt would be an early success. But other times, it all seemed to go wrong, ending in an all-night dog pursuit.

The worst thing for a hound owner was when their dog would run after a deer or some other fast-moving animal that, first of all, isn't a coon, and second of all, can cover a few miles in a very short amount of time. When that happened, it meant we might as well trade in our boots for a pair of jogging shoes.

Marathon, anyone?

Of course, there was some joy to be found in walking across the fields at night trying to figure out exactly which direction our dogs' barking was coming from. But the possible obstacles were always what lurked in my mind. You never knew when you would come to a swampy wood that needed a detour or walk through an area with an electric fence. It gave you a healthy respect for a well-timed mystery.

You never knew what you would find inside a hotwired area. What if it was there because of a big, vicious bull? Sometimes, a curious herd of cattle could give coon hunters a run in the night. But, no matter what happened or how convinced I was that I'd never go again, the next time the opportunity arose, I was right there to give it my all.

Chewing tobacco was one habit that never struck my fancy, but it wasn't because I didn't try it. It was definitely because I did.

One of the coon-hunting joys was when we all loaded into the neighbor's truck. We would normally make a stop at the local convenience store to get snacks and drinks for the evening hunt.

One night, I decided to try chewing tobacco. It was a cool evening in early October, the beginning of the coon hunting season, and we had a special night planned. We were headed to the river bottom where the coons were hefty and bountiful. Going to the river bottom meant one other thing. Deer! They were also plentiful, and I was pretty sure their legs were a bit longer than nature intended. We all knew that if one of the hounds decided to chase one of these long-legged rascals, we were in for another lengthy night. Therefore, I was convinced I need something extra for the hunt. A treat.

I conned one of the adult hunters into buying a can of snuff for me. I couldn't let my older brothers see it or they would take it from me. So, after we got started on the highway, I slowly pulled the can from my pocket, cracked the lid, and smiled as I inhaled the smell of the wintergreen tobacco.

What could possibly go wrong? Maybe chewing would wind up being a hidden talent.

I dipped into the can and shoved a giant pinch inside my bottom lip—off to the side where all the cool guys put it. There I sat, waiting for the joy to begin.

Suddenly, there was more to this good-smelling stuff than I was prepared for. An intense stinging sensation began prodding my lip. The wintergreen flavored tobacco felt like an arctic blast had exploded in my mouth, but at the same time it burned like fire against the tender skin.

And this is supposed to be cool?

Finally, after it became entirely unbearable, I decided my tongue would serve well to slide it to the other side of my mouth. But that didn't go so well either since fine cut tobacco floats when surrounded by saliva.

There should be a disclaimer on cans for rookies.

At that point, the tobacco and its juice began swimming across my taste buds. Now what? I was trapped behind the driver of an extended cab Chevy truck with seven other guys. They were all in their normal buzz of conversation, and I was in absolute misery. What was I supposed to do?

I knew these men well enough to know that if I told them what I'd done and the condition I was in, I would be a laughingstock for months. The swelling amount of tobacco and saliva grew in my mouth like a derelict mudslide of disgusting slime. And after weighing out all my options, I did the unthinkable.

I swallowed.

Yes, all of it slipped down my throat without argument, and I was finally able to breathe a sweet sigh of relief. Perhaps "sweet" is an overstatement.

Yes... yes, definitely an overstatement.

Without warning, my stomach began to churn and my head swam with dizziness. I was sick! Sicker than I had ever been—in recent memory.

When we finally got to the clearing, I bolted out of the truck and into the fresh, redeeming air.

Crisis averted.

I never really had much desire for chewing after that.

It was just a little too extreme.

PLAIN LESSON FOR LIFE

Consider Your Fuel Source

As a youngster, there was nothing that tickled my fancy more than getting to go to the local convenient store, especially after a hot day on the farm. The two-mile trip from home would take about fifteen minutes in the buggy, and after tying Star to the hitching post, we made our way inside and straight to what we were after—the white and blue lighted 'Fountain Drinks' sign.

Grabbing a thirty-two ounce Styrofoam cup, I filled it with ice then pressed the lever to unleash the freezing beverage that I was convinced could quench the Mojave Desert.

A few years later, the scene was much the same as before. We would scrape together whatever change we could find around the house, then head to the same store. But now, the objective was completely different.

I can still see us standing there peering across the counter, handing the clerk a one-dollar bill (despite her obvious skepticism), and walking away with a pack of generic brand cigarettes. I was barely in my double-digits, and yes, that was before the age restriction for buying tobacco was in place. The good ole days!

But we don't have to be very old before we realize that there is a raging thirst within us—an innate desire to be filled. Only the reasons change with time.

Like a young sailor with dreams of a distant land, we cut the rope and push off into the ocean of life determined to find that *something* that our heart cries out for. Sadly, it's a futile attempt.

Fountain drinks and cigarettes may hit the spot temporarily, but they have no real ability to fill the void left by excluding God. Yes, it feels good to our taste buds for a brief moment, but within mere seconds, we thirst again.

No matter how vile or sincere our intentions, the result is the same—the raging want continues.

A few years ago, my son was mowing the lawn. Eventually, the mower ran out of gas. After finding both gas cans empty, my son decided to improvise, wanting to please me by having it all done by the time I got home.

Pleased with his alternative fuel source, he filled up the mower, pulled the starter rope, but nothing happened. He tried again and again, but with no success. Exhausted, he lumbered into the house, defeated.

When I arrived home, I found a very disappointed young man. I could feel his frustration as he told me what had happened. Then I decided to check the mower's gas tank for myself, and found it was filled with water!

Though my son had good intentions and worked very hard, it didn't change the fact that the designer of that little mower engine created it to run on a specific fuel—gasoline.

Ponder the following points as you consider your fuel source:

- Our Creator designed us to live in a loving relationship with Him
- There's only one thing that can truly satisfy our need—Living Water
- We can receive fulfillment by faith through prayer

Jesus stood and cried, saying, "If any man thirst, let him come unto me and drink. He that believeth on me, as the scripture hath said, out of his belly shall flow rivers of living water" (John 7:b37-38).

Chapter Seven

A SHEATH FOR THE PAST

Though it happened over thirty years ago, its images in my mind and its scars on my psyche are as clear as the lines on my own face.

I was six years old and though I don't specifically remember what I was doing, but I was likely meandering around or playing with my toys in the sandbox.

The events of the day unfolded in such a way that there was a young adult that called my name and said he needed my help with something. Feeling a boost of pride and importance, I sprinted off to find him and help where I could. I followed his voice and found him in a small building located off the side of the barn. After receiving instructions, I tackled the job with gusto.

Finally, the task was completed and with a feeling of true satisfaction, I readied to leave the building.

Then I noticed something strange—his behavior. His very peculiar behavior.

He spoke kindly and calmly as he demonstrated for me what he wanted me to do.

Why is he doing this?

I quietly followed his instructions as he indulged in what he wanted. Gratification.

Should I feel good, or guilty? I just didn't know.

It only took only a few seconds for me to walk out that day, but it has taken a lifetime to escape what happened to me. I had no idea that what took place—that confusing, disturbing behavior—had a label.

Sexual abuse.

A moment of violation, broken trust, and bewilderment exploded in my life without invitation or warning. I felt a mixture of disgrace and filthiness I couldn't explain. It opened a world to me that God had never intended. I suffered and struggled and fought strongholds over the next two decades that had their roots in what happened in a matter of minutes.

During those years, I hurt many people, some intentionally and others, not. Either way, as I remember the offenses, I try to take the opportunity to make amends.

I didn't understand at the time, but now I realize that victims somehow carry a sense of ownership for the disgrace felt, as if they were the ones who did something wrong. Silence and loneliness occur, and the victim rarely speaks out for fear that no one will believe them.

This experience spun me into a life of sexual immorality and inappropriate behavior with myself and those around me—a life that God never intended for a young lad to experience. Consequently, the heap of guilt, shame, and lust rose higher and higher until finally I felt I would never be free.

Did my parents know? Absolutely not. They would have been horrified. I never told anyone what happened until years later.

Now, after all those years have passed, I'm glad to say that God has brought much healing to me, but I never dreamed the process would be so slow. Today, I pity the predator far more than myself, since the chances are that, somewhere in their life, someone had taken advantage of them, as well. They may have never found freedom, forgiveness, and healing from their own experience.

One of the biggest lies that victims believe is that if they ignore the reality of what happened to them and never talk about it, somehow, it will eventually go away. But it doesn't. It can't. And it never will. Like a leech, it will suck the life from its victim until it's dealt with—for good.

This is perhaps where my spiritual journey began—like someone unleashed a war within me. I started sensing a battle for my soul between a dark side filled with fear, anger and bitterness. But I also felt a hunger to know and understand God. I began thinking about Bible stories I'd learned, and things I'd heard the Amish preachers say.

Something began to grow inside me, and I purposed to start reading the German Bible every night and to kneel by my bedside and say the Lord's Prayer before going to sleep. This brought some relief against the war that raged in my soul, but no matter what I tried, I always came back to the reality that I was broken.

On the outside, I was enjoying school and experiencing lots of highlights in life, but my private life was sinking lower and lower. Entering the age of puberty brought about another level of struggles that I wasn't sure how to deal with. The inner challenge of my true identity and degradation kept growing stronger, and at a young age I became a slave to masturbation.

I found physical momentary relief and satisfaction, but it was always followed by more perversion and hideous feelings in my heart.

Yet, during this time, my hunger and desire to know God continued to grow. In a neighboring wood, there was a teepee my brothers and I had built. I enjoyed going there whenever I could just to be alone. My desperation to know God brought me to a point of decision.

I knew God existed, but I needed proof.

I prayed, "Lord, if you are real, I pray you will strike me blind right now!"

I squeezed my eyes shut tight, waited for a bit, and then opened them slowly to see if He had answered my prayer.

The fact was, I wasn't blind and likely never would be. I didn't even wear glasses.

Thank God for unanswered prayers!

† † †

I was eleven years old when the horse collar manufacturing company my dad was working for came up for sale. Uncle Roman was ready to let it go, and Dad was very interested in taking it off his hands. Over the years, I had cherished every opportunity to go with Dad to his work, and I was excited about the idea of my family owning the business!

It sounded so important and promising.

Finally, the announcement was made that the Rabers would buy the company, keeping the name the same: Southern Indiana Collar Mfg.

Years before this, Dad had built a 50-foot by 200-foot poultry barn, but due to the sinking economy, the building had been sitting empty for a long time. It was the perfect space. We went to work right away, remodeling the barn and making all the necessary changes to convert it to the shop Dad needed. We poured a lot of concrete, built interior walls, prepared mounting brackets for heavy machinery, and wired lights.

When the day came to start moving all the heavy machines from Uncle Roman's shop to ours, Dad hired local taxi drivers with trucks and trailers, and others who had tractors and wagons.

And the moving commenced.

I don't know exactly how long it took, only that there was a lot of heavy lifting and machinery that had to be put into place. My dad and older brothers worked long and hard to accomplish the mission. Finally, it was all finished. We were ready for business!

The only two experienced employees were my dad and my uncle, John Henry Knepp. But the rest of us were eager to learn. Dad, Uncle John, Ken, Olen, and me were the new Southern Indiana Collar work crew.

We started with an all-natural, high-quality side of cow hide leather, tanned to perfection. We pulled the correct pattern from the large shelf and began cutting numerous patterns to form the pieces needed to make the horse collar. A heavy-duty sewing machine was used to sew the collars together, and then they were put on a rack for lacing.

That was my department!

I placed the collar in an old wooden vice, strapped it down tight, and began the work of lacing. The outside seam of the collar, although already sewn, needed to be reinforced. The holes were pre-punched with a machine but needed to be reamed out with a leather awl and then hand-stitched with strips of leather rawhide. The average size collar had a grand total of eighty-seven stitches. When the day was done, my aching fingers bemoaned every single one of them.

At first, I attacked the job with vigor, and couldn't have been more excited to be a part of the new family endeavor. But after a while, the exhilaration wore off and the job turned tiresome.

Very tiresome.

With the attention span only my decade long life would allow, I was sure the ho-hum of my stitching in and out was going to drive me completely mad.

There were lots of benefits to having a leather shop, one being we could make all kinds of special things from scrap pieces of hide.

One day I was doing just that. I had gotten a knife from the local Flea Market and wanted to make a sheath for it. So, I went to work finding the exact piece I needed. We were allowed to do such things, but Dad always warned us to be careful around all the sharp tools, and to be especially mindful when using the heavy machines.

It was on a Saturday when Dad happened to be caring for a customer while I was working on the knife sheath. The progress was coming along well, and I was almost finished, but I needed a tool from the shelf above the table. And since I was too short to reach it, I jumped up and knelt on the table to grab it.

Retrieving it, I hopped back down and continued my work. A few minor tweaks and I was all done. With a satisfied feeling, I ran to Dad who was still caring for a customer.

"Look what I made!" I said, beaming with joy.

Dad was examining my sheath when the customer exclaimed, "What is that on your foot, Son?"

I looked down at my bare feet and saw my left foot was covered in blood!

As I bent over for a closer look, I noticed my pants had a tiny slit right by the knee. One of Dad's commonly used tools was a draw knife, and it had a blade that protruded up from its frame, nice and sharp. It was used for cutting thick leather.

That knife had been lying on the table when I jumped from the shelf. In my enthusiasm, I didn't see it and knelt right onto the blade, sinking it deep into my knee.

Like so many things that test and try us—peculiar behavior and knives that cut deep—can take only a few seconds to injure, but the scars they leave can linger forever.

The pain is now long gone both physically and emotionally, but I bear the abrasions to this very day.

Chapter Eight

CHASING DREAMS

I wanted a boat!

One with an outboard motor and a steering wheel. The older I got, the more I was obsessed with the dream.

I would have happily settled for any 10′ Aluminum Jon boat and a 5 to 10 horsepower outboard engine, preferably a Mercury—the kind with the steering handle attached right to the engine. You drive it from the back. Not nearly as cool as the ones with a steering wheel, but at that point, anything that had an engine and ran meant I actually wouldn't be using oars!

I'd like to think my expectations weren't too high, and the only obstacle standing in my way was trying to figure out how to talk Dad into funding my ambition. And it didn't go well. Let's just say that it was a very short conversation.

Still, it didn't detour me the least little bit. I thought maybe I could find a free one, so I searched the newspapers and kept a close eye out anytime we went somewhere outside the community. The more time that passed, the less picky I became about what I was looking for. Anything would be better than nothing. Then it hit me.

I would build my own boat!

I knew exactly what I would use. Dad wouldn't give me a few hundred dollars for a real boat, but I was positive he would be impressed with my aspiration and would give me $20 for materials...

... and he did.

I could just see it! It would only be a matter of time, and I would be speeding across the pond in my very own creation! Now I understood how the Wright Brothers or Henry Ford must have felt when dreams finally came to fruition. They were real pioneers, just like me!

I hitched our pony Jim to the buggy, hooked up the trailer that I would need to haul my goods, and drove to a local shop where I knew they would have just what I needed.

"I'd like to buy four 50-gallon, plastic barrels," I said.

They were $5 each. After handing the sales guy the money, we loaded the barrels onto the trailer and I headed for home. The future looked promising. I needed an adult brain and physical power to help me accomplish my goals, and, after some coaxing, my brother Ken agreed. We started working lickety-split. I had waited long enough, and now my vision was within reach!

Finally, we had it completed. A wooden platform approximately 6 feet wide and 8 feet long with four plastic barrels securely fastened underneath, a little wobbly, but we were good to go. I still needed one more thing before I was ready for water: An outboard motor.

Again, Dad rejected the idea of buying one, even the cheapest one I could find. And again, it was time to improvise.

I had a thought, and I was confident my idea would work. Soon, I would be sailing across the water, the wind blowing through my bleach blonde hair. Dad had recently purchased a new weed-eater to replace our old one, which was rickety and hardly ran. But with a little work, this could be the answer.

I blew some of the dust off of it, cleaned out the air filter, and with some persuading and a cloud of smoke, it ran. I was super excited! I loaded it up on the buggy and made the 1½ mile drive to the small engine shop.

"I need to fasten a propeller on the end of this weed eater," I said to the gentleman, feeling like a genuine entrepreneur.

The man looked at me quizzically and said, "Go buy a boat motor."

"I can't do that," I answered, "I don't have that kind of money."

"I'm sorry," he said, "but I'm afraid I can't help you."

Disappointed in his lack of creative insight, I drove home.

For now, I'll just have to try the boat without the motor.

Back at home, Ken and I loaded our newly-built boat onto the trailer and hauled it to the pond a mile away. I could hardly wait. We unloaded it, dragged it down to the water then pushed it just off the shore. The time had come for us to enjoy our handiwork!

I stood in the water and steadied it while Ken jumped in. Then, he helped me board our little vessel. With a 2x4 for an oar, we pushed off the bank and slid into deeper water. I couldn't believe it. There we were, floating on the liquid blue in a craft we had made ourselves.

Unbelievable!

And as we settled into our groove, resting in the floating, bobbing, and rolling sensation of freedom, one of us took the liberty of shifting our body weight. Before we knew what had happened, we capsized our timid vessel and ended up spitting pond water as we swam back to shore.

Disappointed, wet, and embarrassed, we pulled our failed project to land, loaded it on the trailer, and went home to face the laughter and jeers.

I suppose there is a lot to be said about boats, motors, and life in general. It's a balancing act.

†††

What boy doesn't fanaticize about driving—or at least riding in—a big ole semi truck?

The best day that ever came was when I received a call from my first cousin, Sam.

"Hey, Amos!" he said. "How would you like to ride with me in the semi? I have a load going to North Carolina."

I didn't have to think about it for more than a second. "Yes!" I exclaimed.

The anticipation was almost uncontainable! One thing is for sure, there was no forcing needed from Dad at chore time. As a matter of fact, I could hardly wait since that meant it would be so much closer to the time Sam would pick me up.

I bounced energetically from one duty to the next like a cat with balls of yarn. I was on it! Periodically, I would peep through a window or crack in the barn to check if I would see Sam's truck coming. Though it wasn't time for him yet, I could always hope he'd show up early!

With all my daily responsibilities fulfilled, I scampered off to the house to take a shower and pack my clothes. I could hardly believe it—I was going on a long trip in a real semi!

Sure enough and right on time, Sam pulled in the driveway in his little S-10 pickup truck. I said my goodbyes and flew out of the house, and Sam and I were gone! Gone on a long awaited adventure.

† † †

The drive across the community was short, and soon enough we came to a stop in the parking lot beside the big rig. Wow!

My emotions soared as I climbed up into that massive W900 Kenworth. I stared at all the buttons and switches on the dash. It was even better than I had thought! My fascination only grew when Sam turned the key and the immense diesel engine roared to life. It shuddered off to a start as all eighteen wheels began rolling at once. I marveled as Sam smoothly shifted through all thirteen gears.

My imagination, as active as it was, could never have captured all the excitement I was feeling. Back on the farm, I was used to operating the Case or John Deere tractor with four, maybe five gears, but this... this was just too much.

"How much do we weigh," I asked.

"Eighty thousand pounds," Sam replied with a grin.

As we made our way through the community, heading for Highway 50, I gazed at all the familiar farms and places, and even buggies we met with people I recognized. But the world took on a whole new look through the window of an eighteen-wheeler. When we finally made it the highway, turned east, and headed out of our little community, our destination was Wilmington, North Carolina.

We drove into the night, and after several hours the buzz started to wear off. As a young man addicted to smoking since a tender age, I started to feel a bit skittish. I fidgeted nervously as the urge for a cigarette intensified. But I hesitated. Rumor had it that Sam had made a change in his life, and I wasn't even sure what that meant.

We had to make a brief stop by the side of the highway for Sam to check the load, and I decided this was my chance. I got out my cigarettes, lit up, and was basking in the glow when Sam returned. He climbed in and at first said nothing.

Then, he turned to me and softly stated, "I forgot to tell you that I don't allow smoking in my truck."

What could I say? I put it out.

The next day, it was time for a fuel stop in Wilmington, North Carolina. After filling up and checking all the fluids, Sam went into the truck stop to pay for the gasoline. I was bored, and since I couldn't smoke, I thought I'd turn on the radio. After scanning the stations and finding nothing of interest, I found an untitled cassette tape and plugged it into the player.

I expected some kind of music, but to my surprise, it was a man passionately sharing how Jesus had rescued him from sin. As quickly as I could, I turned it off and sat in a lull for a few minutes. Finally, my curiosity got the best of me, and I turned it back on.

I hastily shut it off when I saw Sam approaching.

I had no clue who the speaker was, and it wasn't until years later that the full significance of this experience was revealed.

Somehow, Sam must have known I was listening to it, because he began talking to me about the Bible and sharing verses about God's love. He had picked up two small Gideon Bibles in the truck stop and asked me if I had a personal Bible. He offered one to me and marked a few scriptures in it for me to look at.

This is a bit bizarre. Surely he knows we have several Bibles at home.

I guess the rumors were true. It seemed like Sam really had changed. There was a kindness and tranquility about him that hadn't been there before. Not like this. And it appealed to me.

It was simple, striking, and authentic.

I guess I've learned that everyone has their own version of what a dream looks like, and we can chase them down in many different ways—

with weed-eaters...

eighteen-wheelers...

a man on a cassette tape.

Amos at approximately 14 years old

Chapter Nine

THE ENEMY FROM WITHIN

Regina was kind, compassionate and her joyful personality was accompanied by a contagious giggle. As a young boy trying to model after my three older brothers, I wasn't always sure what to do with an older sister.

I recall her spending time with me, playing games, and telling stories. Since she was the oldest girl, it seemed like she always had a lot of chores to do: mowing the lawn, hoeing the garden, or just the kind of clean up that was required around a farm like ours. I wasn't always willing to help, but normally it didn't take much to change my mind.

"Hey, Amos," she would call from the house. "Would you like to help me with cleaning up today?"

Due to my hesitation, she added, "When we're done, we can sit by the shade tree; I'll have a bag of candy and a special drink for you."

That's all it took.

"I'll do it!"

I was all about being rough and tough and independent, and since she was a girl, she didn't register very high on the cool scale. Yet, there was something about her that I adored. She was soft-spoken, kind-hearted, and cried easier than any boy I had ever met. She also read books to me and went with me on relaxing walks. At night when I wasn't ready to fall asleep, she graciously listened to my endless chatter until my eyelids began to droop.

She was slightly overweight and very self-conscience about it. Unfortunately, my brothers used that as their weapon of choice when teasing or manipulating her. My heart aches with regret at memories of us tormenting her and calling her names.

As a rule, she would try to defend herself, but eventually, as the insults kept coming, she would slowly start to break down and then run away in tears.

I now try to concentrate on my kinder moments and the fun times we had.

Brothers can be creeps.

†††

Spring was bringing changes of a new season, except there seemed to be one variation so subtle, hardly anyone noticed.

It was Regina.

She had been experiencing exhaustion and random bruises on her body, and most noticeably, the color seemed to be gradually draining from her cheeks. Perhaps she needed more sleep or was fighting a flu bug. Maybe she just needed to take her vitamins more consistently?

One night while Regina and I were in the barn milking the cows, we talked about the symptoms she was having. Hesitantly, I asked her what was wrong with her.

She smiled and without hesitation replied, "I'm going to be sick, and then I'm going to die."

What?

Just like that, it had all been laid bare.

Nobody likes the thought of dying, but she just said it out loud. Suddenly, in the same milking barn where we had spent so many evenings singing, laughing, and sharing so many vulnerable years. The warmth was sucked out in a second, leaving it feeling cold and lonely.

In one of the first mowings of that spring, Regina was out walking behind the mower as she had done so many times before. She normally mowed for at least an hour and would then stop for a cool drink and a brief rest before continuing on. On that day, she only seemed to be able to mow for a few minutes, then needed to stop for a rest.

With the mower stopping and starting so frequently, Mom paused her house work to look out the window. There she saw Regina leaning over the trampoline in exhaustion.

"That's it," Mom said. "Something has to be done."

The next day, Mom, Regina, and my sister Leanna made the seven-mile trip in the buggy to the town of Loogootee to see Dr. Sutton.

The news was devastating, and the need for treatment was urgent.

It was Leukemia.

I had never heard that word before, but I knew it was some form of cancer, and I had heard *that* word plenty of times. Most people I knew with cancer gradually wasted away and eventually—inevitably—passed away. My parents silently shed tears as they grieved the reality of this devastating diagnosis.

Regina was young, energetic, and full of life.

Upon doctor's orders, they immediately rushed her to the Daviess County Hospital, but the stay was short. The next morning, they were sent to Indianapolis to start chemotherapy ASAP.

The commotion that filled our home was almost too much. Mom and dad took turns staying at the hospital with her at all times. Their absence served as a continual reminder that something was wrong. At least once a week there would be a van load that would make the two-hour drive to visit. Yes, she looked ill, but at first there were no noticeable changes.

But we all knew what was coming. The chemo therapy that went coursing through her body would kill all the bad cells, but it would kill the good ones, too. She grew very sick, and after the first seven days of chemo were completed, it was time for tests to see if the cancer cells were still present.

They were.

The doctors said three more days of treatment would probably do it and they were right. The tests came back the second time, and she was cancer free!

Regina was officially in remission!

There was still a commotion in our home, but now the atmosphere had changed. There was new hope in the air. After five weeks in the hospital, Regina was coming home!

There was a warmth in my soul; we were all back together again—at home.

I watched in awe as the evening unfolded. The conversation and laughter had returned. I saw every one of my siblings, my mom and dad as they interacted with Regina, each in their own unique way. Though we weren't a family that used an abundance of flowery words, in that moment it was undeniable.

We loved each other.

Then I noticed it.

Wait. Is that what I think it is?

The lantern was casting intermittent shadows in the room, so I squinted my eyes for a closer look.

It is...

There was a small spot on the side of her head. It was obvious that she had tried to comb her brunette hair in a way to hide it just like she had tried to hide her bruises, but it was irrefutable. Regina was losing her hair.

As a side effect of the chemo therapy treatments, we all knew it was coming and it lingered in the back of our minds like a thunder storm moving in from the west.

Regina had embraced the reality and was trying to prepare herself for it. She had found loose hair in her bed while at the hospital and knew it would only get worse. She would eventually be completely bald. Her stay at home would be one week before she needed to go back for additional tests and another seven days of chemo.

One morning, she asked my mother to take her into a side room and comb her hair, in private. Mom hesitated slightly knowing precisely what this meant. She took the comb and slowly lifted it to her dear daughter's head, gently moving the comb through her auburn strands. As another side effect of the treatments, it was stiff and sticky. And as expected, Regina's hair began coming out. At first, in thin ribbons, then in clumps until finally it was all gone. Her head was as smooth as butter. Mom's eyes fell to the hair on the floor, the clumps in her hand.

Mama went for a stroll through her archive of mental snapshots. She reminisced about the little clump of hair Regina had when she was born, and the excitement when it was long enough to braid for the very first time. Then, how it grew and matured along with Regina as she developed into a fine young woman. Now, due to this horrid disease called cancer and the aggressive medications, the once pretty ornament was reduced to a lifeless blob on the floor. Instead of a comb, she now needed a broom, a dust pan, and trash can to put it in.

Regina turned and walked aimlessly toward the bathroom where she looked in the mirror and saw herself as if for the first time. After several minutes, she returned to the living room to join Mom.

"The important thing is that I get well," she said with a glimmer of hope. "The hair will come back after that."

All too soon, her one week stay at home was over and it was time to go back for her final round of chemo. But it was different this time. We all knew the cancer was in remission and that gave us hope and a lot to be grateful for.

Still, Mom and Dad were advised to take my sister to Juarez, Mexico for some additional natural treatment to build up her immune system. After so much chemotherapy, Regina's fragile body was depleted and drained.

On July 11th, they made the 1,500-mile trip to cross the border for three weeks of treatments. It was with a mix of emotions that we all said our goodbyes.

Yes, we would miss them tremendously, but it didn't seem as daunting now that we knew my big sister's cancer was on its way out.

The next three weeks seemed like an eternity, but at last the day came when we saw the van traveling down the dirt road toward our house. It slowed and turned into our driveway, and they were home! Mom, Dad, Regina, and my little sister LeAnna were now safely back from Mexico.

In the midst of all the heaviness our family was enduring, there was at least one bright spot.

Cards!

Lots and lots of greeting cards poured in from our community and others. Many of them included money to help my parents pay for the hospital bills that started piling up. A string of bright and beautiful cards hung from one side of the house to the other, and still there was not enough room for them all.

Though my sister would soon be undergoing what we all thought was the final leg of her recovery, my mind still played out all the possibilities of what might happen. The thoughts were overwhelming.

I was scared.

I was scared for her—of the enemy from within.

Chapter Ten

A BRAVE ATTEMPT

As I watched my sister Regina struggle with Leukemia, I hit an all-time low of loneliness and discouragement.

I had a strong sense that the only way to rise above the pain was to end my life.

It wasn't a new idea.

I had contemplated it often. But how would I actually do it? Then, an idea. We had a Harrison Richardson .22 caliber pistol that my brother Ken had bought from my uncle, which had belonged to a retired policeman.

That would be my weapon to freedom.

I carefully thought through every detail, making sure it was going to work. Finally, I was satisfied and ready to execute my plan.

I would get up during the night and ride our pony Jim back to the teepee. There, away from anyone who might stop me, I would put a bullet in my head. But there was only one possible glitch that could ruin it all. I was the one who did the chores and let the horses into the field for the night. If I wanted to use Jim, I'd have to keep him in the barn, since catching him in the field at night would be nearly impossible.

Dad always made his round through the barn before bedtime, and he would surely find him. So, I hid him in a stall we hadn't been using and hoped for the best.

It was an ordinary day with the usual responsibilities, but it was also a sad day—it was my last day on earth.

That afternoon, I noticed when LeAnna arrived home from school. I watched her from the barn as she walked carelessly to the house, her lunch pail swinging from her hand. I loved her so dearly. Like all siblings, we had our typical rivalries, but at the end of the day, she was my sister and I adored her.

Olen, my brother next oldest to me, and I had chores we always did together. For him it was just another evening of mundane responsibilities; he had no idea what I had been planning. When we finished our jobs together, he walked away without a word. I lingered, turned slowly to watch him as he left the barn. Out of all my siblings, we had probably spent the most time together—playing together as children, working as young men, and riding our ponies freely across the open fields.

My daydreaming was interrupted by the sound of a pickup truck pulling up in the driveway. I knew without looking that it was my two oldest brothers coming home from their daily construction job. I heard voices, the truck door slam, and the truck roaring back out of our driveway. Marlin was my oldest brother. He wasn't the life of a party, but he was rock solid and strong as an ox, and I admired him for that.

Ken, the second oldest boy in the family, was probably my favorite. He was tall, not as strong as Marlin although they were continually testing their strength one against the other. Ken was the primary hunter of our clan and maintaining good favor with him was of upmost importance. It meant more hunting privileges. He was also the athletic one of the pack, able to dunk a ten-footer.

"Come in for supper!" came the long-winded call from the house.

We all gathered around the table in our usual places. Dad's summon to pray came in the form of a slight shuffle. It was the mealtime routine. We had all been taught from childhood to clasp our hands on our laps and bow in silence. And again, the same slight shuffle was repeated when the prayer time was over.

I don't remember what we ate that evening, but I'm sure it was one of Mom's delicious meals. What came after supper was as predictable as clock work. Mom bustled around the kitchen, cleaning up while Dad sat in his recliner—shoes and socks off—resting his feet from a hard day, his face hid behind the daily Times Herald or the Budget.

I could have been doing any number of things: reading, playing a game, or trying to talk Dad into breaking out his harmonica. But on that particular night, in the most inconspicuous manner possible, I wandered outside...

... on a mission.

When it felt safe and unsuspicious, I darted for the barn to see if my horse Jim had successfully gone unidentified during Dad's evening walkthrough.

But Jim was still there. My plan was on.

At the normal 9:00pm bedtime, I said my goodnights to my mom and dad, then slowly climbed the stairs, glancing one last time at them before disappearing from sight.

My dad...though I rarely remember being caressed or comforted by his callused hands, I knew he loved me. It was the little teasing remarks and the wink of his eye that expressed love to me. I enjoyed his laughter and sense of humor, but above all, he was my greatest inspiration for music.

Now my mom...she had given birth to me, nursed me in my infancy, and helped me take those first steps as a toddler. I spent countless hours playing on the floor while she sat and sewed clothes for the family with her old fashion peddle sewing machine. Her feet rocked back and forth as the needle and walker zipped across the fabric. She'd lovingly run her fingers through my hair with that passionate touch as she smiled and called me her "sonny boy". Then there was the first day of school when she stood and waved to me at the end of our long lane.

Do I really want to go through with this?

Distressed but determined, I set my alarm for 11:30pm. After sliding a bullet into the chamber of the revolver, I tucked it away safely and climbed into bed.

I lay there in the stillness of the night as the quietness deafened me. The curtain waved lightly as a gentle breeze carried in all the sounds hidden in the dark. I could hear the insects, the farm animals, and the occasional car as it passed by on our little gravel road.

Finally, I drifted off.

When the alarm woke me from a restless sleep, it was go-time. Everyone else in the house was sound asleep as I got dressed and hurried over to the dresser to get the revolver. My hand slid silently under the lumps of clothing in the drawer until my fingers touched the cool steel barrel. I wavered for a second, but then grabbed it and headed out.

As I reached for the latch and opened the door, I looked out at the night sky. It was so big, clear, and lit by a glimmering moon surrounded by millions of stars.

I suddenly sensed a Presence I had never felt before. And as I tried to move, I couldn't seem to get through the door. I just stood there, frozen, feeling that invisible Presence that was undeniably there and all too real. My brave attempt at suicide had been under minded.

Did I just meet God?

I turned and went back to bed.

Though my troubles and struggles didn't by any means disappear—not for the next few years—that night changed my soul forever. I had experienced something...

... something more powerful than I had ever known.

Beyond my grasp.

Chapter Eleven

A MESSENGER IN THE NIGHT

The paramedics came and quickly tended to us, and soon our empty field was swarming with people. I watched as the fire department pried Amanda out of the SUV and carried her toward the ambulance on a stretcher.

I followed close behind fully intending to ride with her, but they insisted we ride separately so they could care for us individually.

The ride to the hospital seemed longer than it should have. I guess when life gets boiled down to its essence, it slows in order for us to grasp what's truly important—to hang on to it as long as possible.

†††

As a young teen, my love for singing and playing harmonica

continued to grow. I carried the gift my father gave me in my pants pocket in case of a spare moment or even a job around the farm I could do with one hand while playing it with the other. It also came in handy for personal entertainment while traveling, whether locally in a buggy or long-distance to another Amish community.

During this time, my dad bought a swing set from some local people, and their sons came out to install it. One of those sons was a young man who would become one of my best friends, Jeff Miller. We shared the same love of music and singing, and he played a few different stringed instruments. When I turned sixteen, I aspired to buy a guitar and learn how to play.

I went to the local general store and bought a new but cheap six-string for $89. Jeff supplied me with some basic chord and strumming techniques, and I went to work. I played for hours, convinced that I would never get my fingers to bend in the odd shapes I saw Jeff's bend while he played. But I had to keep trying.

"You need to be able to put your fingers in the right place without looking," Jeff said.

Impossible, I thought.

But I worked long and hard, and even though it seemed like an eternity, in less than a week I was playing my first song. It was rough and far from soothing, but I didn't care. I did it!

Jeff and I ended up spending hours together enthralled as we learned new songs. His entire family was talented musically, and over time, we began our own little a cappella group singing four-part harmony. It wasn't long before invitations came in for us to perform around the community. We sang for elderly folks, at birthday parties, and even at weddings.

It felt so natural to me, like I had finally found my calling.

† † †

Regina's Leukemia had been in remission for the past few years, and my family was enjoying life again. My brothers Marlin and Ken were both married by now, and my mom and dad were loving being grandparents. I was certainly enjoying the nieces and nephews.

Everything was good.

The month was September and fall was rapidly approaching. Our family was in bed and peacefully sleeping when suddenly, the night was interrupted by the sound of a pickup truck speeding up our gravel driveway. It came skidding to a stop as someone emerged and came running toward the house yelling for my dad.

Dad flew to the door as the messenger frantically informed him that my older brother, his wife, and two children were in a terrible accident. I remember the fear and confusion as Mom and Dad swiftly awoke some of the older kids to tell them what had happened.

After grabbing a few necessities, they ran to the truck and it roared out of the driveway. The rest of us—just ripped out of a deep sleep—were left reeling with never ending questions.

What had happened? Were they going to be okay? Did someone die?

No one, not even the messenger, seemed to know any details.

Conversation was sparse as my parents raced through the community. Gripping the wheel tightly, the driver stared straight ahead, only loosening his fingers to adjust his mirrors. The last thing he needed was to be noticed by some ambitious cop in wait for a reckless driver.

Mom and Dad's second born son Kenneth, his wife Marianna, and their two children weighed heavy on their minds.

Dear Lord, please keep them safe.

As the truck crested a knob, they saw the EMS speeding toward them, the flashing lights were blinding as they met and then listened as the screaming siren faded in the distance. Gathering their thoughts, they slowed down, turned, and followed the ambulance that carried its precious cargo.

Back at the house, the night was restless. Morning finally came and, like any other, the chores needed to be done. The animals didn't seem to be affected by all the chaos. The big horses came into the barn from the fields with their never-ending appetites. The cows were just as naughty as ever, taking any opportunity they could to kick the buckets as we worked to fill them with fresh milk.

After the chores were all done, we sat around the table for the breakfast Regina had made. Oh, I was so grateful she wasn't sick anymore. Her complexion and strength had been steady now for a little over three years, and the doctors were pleased with her overall condition.

Instead of the normal chatter that morning, there was a dull stillness as we all contemplated our new reality. Only the ringing of the telephone broke the silence.

It was Dad calling from the hospital. We all scrambled around the speaker so we could hear first-hand what he said.

First, he wanted to make sure everything at the farm was okay. After that, his voice dropped.

"The doctors say Ken's back is broken and they're preparing for surgery right now." His voice splintered with emotion.

With that, the anticipation in the room drained out. I meandered off to finish a chore I had left for later. Olen walked introspectively over to the window and gazed blankly out across the fields.

Myron, my eighteen month old nephew, and Marsha, my little niece who was only five months old, escaped the accident with only a few minor bruises and scratches. Ken and his wife Marianna, however, remained in a coma for the next ten days.

But surely they would both be alright.

†††

Ken had been 14 years old when he persuaded Dad to give him $75 for a coonhound. He purchased a full-blooded Walker pup and named her Dolly. Thus started the Raber family coon adventures we all loved for the next two decades.

When the heavens were right and the hounds were ready, I could still see Ken standing there listening then proudly announcing when he could identify Dolly's bark from amongst all the other howling hounds. She was a family favorite, and we still treasure lots of coon hunting memories with her. She died on the farm at age 13, and the hunters in the family gathered, dug a grave, and gave her a proper burial.

But she was Ken's dog...

†††

Several more tests would be needed before Ken's condition was eventually confirmed: He was paralyzed from his waist down.

My brother was officially a paraplegic.

I simply couldn't believe it; none of us could. I admired Ken so much and couldn't imagine what he must have been feeling. He was tall, strong, energetic, and had so much zeal for life.

My heart ached as I realized the implications this could have on his young family, the entire extended family, and our community. I was his proud little brother that loved to watch and cheer for him from the sideline as he played basketball with the neighborhood boys. His protégé of thrilling outdoor life—fishing, trapping, and coon hunting.

My mind raced as I tried to make some sense of all the changes that were coming. Ken and Marianna had been married for just over three years, and it was only two years ago that family and neighbors had come together to build the house for the new couple.

Now, life had flipped upside down.

Family members took turns staying at the hospital while others stayed home and cared for the farm and the horse collar business. Each day, we waited for the news, eager to see how Ken and Marianna were doing. Marianna finally recovered and helped where she could, but Ken's condition stayed unstable for weeks.

After four weeks in the local hospital, the decision was made that Ken would be transferred to Mayo Clinic in Rochester Minnesota. The local doctors had exhausted all their options and the medical teams and specialists there could possibly offer him something more.

The problem was, how were we going to get him there? In his fragile state, there was no way Ken could endure the ten-hour drive. So, after some debate and getting the blessing of Bishop Ben, the decision was made. They would fly.

This was a big deal since aircrafts were/are certainly a luxurious modern convenience, and most Amish churches don't allow their members to fly. But, in the given situation, it was allowed. Ken and my dad would go.

Tickets for two were purchased, and we took them to the International Airport in Evansville, Indiana. We unloaded their luggage and waved goodbye as Dad pushed Ken's wheelchair up the ramp toward the plane.

And again, the waiting game.

What would the doctors at Mayo Clinic say? Perhaps they would find some new hope the local physicians had missed. After all, they were specialists. Day after day, the phone calls came with no real change. The rehabilitation team there was ready to start teaching Ken how to live as a paraplegic, getting used to a wheelchair and caring for himself.

It was October 26th when Ken and Dad packed their bags to come home. It had been nearly eight weeks since the tragic accident, and Ken hadn't been home since that fateful night.

Initially, I was excited. But then reality set in. Coming home? Home to what? His job? His house? The one we had just built for him and his bride and where he was starting a family?

In spite of the turmoil, that difficult day arrived when the van pulled into his driveway. The wheelchair was removed from the back of the van and brought up to the passenger seat. Some strong man—probably one of my older brothers—helped Ken into his chair. Then, for the very first time, my big brother approached his home... sitting.

We helped him through the door as he grieved without a sound. Wheeling himself across the living room floor, emotions ran high for all of us as we felt the pain of this young family. I would have to come to terms with it in my own heart.

We would do everything we could to make his life feel as normal as possible—despite that messenger in the night.

Chapter Twelve

IT'S BACK

Regina was now twenty-two and having a great time cancer-free. Her strength was nearly what it had been before, and she was no longer bald. Her head was covered with an abundance of lovely hair!

Though she still underwent monthly visits to Dr. Sutton, we continued to believe she was cured, and each month we were relieved to hear good news.

She was doing well.

But the continual exhaustion that had once plagued her had returned; as evident as the grey, cloudy hue that covered her cheeks. Like a storm that suddenly comes up behind you with gale-force winds and pelting rain knocking you off our feet... Regina knew it, and so did Mom and Dad.

Regina had called Mr. Bateman, the local Amish taxi driver, to take her to Dr. Sutton's office. I can only imagine the ride—a gorgeous spring day with God's nature in full glory. As they drove along through the countryside, the sun shone in through the window as a balmy breeze caressed her face. God's goodness was all around.

All around.

After her appointment for the usual tests that would inevitably come back normal, Regina sat patiently in the waiting room for the results.

"Regina Rose Raber" called the nurse.

Regina followed the nurse back into the examination room, and since she had made monthly visits there for the past four years, I'm sure she was no stranger to the staff.

Dr. Sutton came in and sat down across from her in his usual place.

"Regina, I'm very sorry..." he said. "The cancer is back. And I'm afraid it is advanced and aggressive."

Only my sister knows what was going through her head when she heard those words.

My sister and God.

It was exactly four years to the date that she was first diagnosed. The news was shocking as the family was still reeling from Ken's accident and his confinement to a wheelchair.

How would everyone deal with all this?

When Regina came home that April day, she told my parents that she wasn't going to do any more chemo therapy or medical treatments. Instead, she wanted to see a naturopath.

When Mom and Dad heard Regina's wishes, they made the trip that afternoon to a herbal physician. Over the next few weeks, her appetite dwindled, but she faithfully continued swallowing the prescribed capsules the best she could—little sips of water that would sometimes nearly cause her to vomit due to the number of pills she would have to take.

I'd just had my sixteenth birthday in February of that year, and I was now officially in the Rumspringa. I joined the other Amish youth on

Wednesday nights and weekends. Normally, at that stage of a young man's life, you'd think I'd be fired up to join my friends, but many times I was hesitant.

And when I went, there was a mixed response from my peers. While awkward and unsure of what to say or do, some were sincerely kind and caring. But others made snide comments, also probably from an ineptness that came with social inexperience.

What do you say to a friend whose sister is dying?

Then a weekend came when all the youth were getting their shiny buggies from the shed to drive to the Sunday night singing. It was difficult to leave the house to go have fun when there were so many unknowns left at home.

Still, it was good to get out and free my mind for a while.

The food was good, the singing and time with my friends created a light mood, and I left with a satisfied feeling. Even the trip home was pleasant as I enjoyed the serenity of the night, the view of the big sky dotted with stars, and the methodical sound of the clip-clop of Star, my horse.

But as we came around the bend and my home came into view, I spotted an ambulance parked in front with its emergency lights flashing. Suddenly, it sped down the driveway, passed me, spitting gravel as it rushed out of sight.

I raced my horse and buggy up the lane to find our neighbors collecting in the drive. They said that my mother had experienced seizures.

Another brick tossed into the family fire pit of troubles.

My poor mother... while she was trying to meet everyone's needs, she neglected to deal with her own.

Grief. Stress. Stomach ulcers.

That night after everyone had left, I stood alone in our front yard looking up into the vast sky. I felt so tiny under all the stars, finding the

Big Dipper and the Little Dipper, both of which I had met through a telescope as a child. But now, things looked differently than they had an hour earlier.

The singing had stopped.

As I stood there, I realized that I had four family members in the hospital within a very short time. My brother and his ongoing physical issues, my sister with Leukemia, my dad with a hernia, and now my mother with stomach ulcers.

What was happening to us?

These were the kind of stories we would occasionally hear from other communities—about other people. We sympathized with them for a few minutes, then continued on with our lives. But this wasn't them, it was us!

Our family.

Where was God and why was He allowing all this to happen? Was He angry with us? What else could be on the way? Would something happen to me next?

The harassing questions were relentless as I tried to move forward as normally as I could.

The first few days were the hardest. The first night was unbearable. During the daytime, everyone would be bustling around with the usual chores and responsibilities with the occasional call for us to rise up and serve in places where there was a void. The difficult part came when night fell and the house seemed to whisper my woes.

As I laid there for what seemed like hours watching the flickering of the oil lamp as it cast shadows on the bedroom door, the only interruption would come from the occasional howl of Sport, our farm dog.

Could he sense what was coming?

Chapter Thirteen

HOLDING UP THE LADDER

Regina's resilience made me treasure her as a sister all the more. She read and re-read cards that came in from friends and family; she sang as much as she could, and always requested prayer with the family before bedtime.

We would kneel in the living room by the couch or wherever we were sitting and listen as Dad prayed a German prayer from the little black prayer book. Even though I didn't understand the words, these times were sacred and very special. Our circumstances were unpredictable and strained, but it was in those moments that brought security and peace to my heart.

I can still see her as she walked around the property with her cane. It seemed like she was reliving memories—a preface to saying her goodbyes. She didn't talk much, but I remember her smile. She looked tired and weary, but still had a ready smile for each of us.

During our conversation in the milking barn four years earlier, she spoke so candidly of her probable death.

She had been so calm, so quiet... so fearless.

I had only two sisters—Regina, and the baby of the family, LeAnna. Sharing a bedroom for the last few years had been a real bonding time for them. LeAnna told us later that they had spent many hours just talking. Regina would confide in her, and without fail before bedtime, would kneel together and talk to Jesus.

Her walks got slower and shorter until the day came when she was no longer able to do anything but lie still.

There's power in stillness.

One evening after chores, I came into the house to find Mom and Dad sitting by the couch where Regina was resting. Since Leukemia is a blood cancer, the body produces an abnormal amount of white blood cells that interfere with or even attack the red blood cells. Since the red blood cells are the carriers of oxygen, excessive bleeding starts when they are weakened or diminished. And Regina had been losing too much blood and was getting weaker.

Too exhausted to make it outside on her own, Regina walked out to the taxi cab leaning heavily on Dad's arm. Slowly, carefully, she got in, and Mom and Dad took her away.

I stood and watched as they disappeared over the small hill on the dirt road, leaving behind nothing but a ribbon of dust and a house of sadness.

Regina spent one week in the hospital, and we had time for some last visits filled with stories and nostalgia. In one of her last moments, she asked my mother and grandmother to hold her hand, and she sang the song, "They're Holding Up the Ladder."

And in those loving hands, she stayed awhile longer.

† † †

The men of the family had been waiting to go coon hunting but kept putting it off just in case Regina's situation worsened. Out in the middle of the woods—running after dogs—while Regina was in the hospital seemed like too big of a risk.

But after Dad had a phone conversation with Mom who was at the hospital, the consensus was that she was doing better, and we shouldn't miss our hunt. Besides, if something should go wrong, they would just call the cell phone of our coon hunting friend.

We loaded the dogs in Gary's truck and headed for our routine snack and drink stop before going to the woods. Everyone tried to act normal, but there was an undeniable heaviness in the air. Not long after we had started hunting, there came a slight drizzle. The air was cold and damp.

"Not much luck here," said one of the hunters. "Let's move on to somewhere else."

We came to the second place and had just let the dogs loose when the phone rang. We all stiffened with fear.

After Gary answered and listened for just a few brief seconds, he handed the phone to Olen, motioning that we needed to leave at once.

We were told to meet our neighbor in Montgomery at the gas station and he would take the three of us to the hospital. Gary would then take the hounds back home to the kennel.

As I sat in the back seat nearly numb with dread, I stared out the windshield as a fine mist began to cover the glass before the wipers took it all away. It reminded me of life over the past few years. Just about the time one bit of chaos settled, something else would hit the windshield of daily existence, clouding everything all over again.

Things just kept changing.

Is her time to leave really here? I wondered. *And what will I say to her if it is?*

It was the longest ride of my life.

When we finally got there, Olen and I raced from the parking lot toward the hospital entrance, found the elevator, and made our way to the third floor.

Would I have the time to thank her for being a good sister? Thank her for all the candy she had given me as a young lad? Would I hold her hand and tell her that I loved her? What would she look like? Would she remember me?

In the waiting room, we were met by a relative. She couldn't speak, but her face said it all. That lonely, agonizing, trembling look as if to say, *you're too late.*

Was life in such a hurry to leave? Did it not look over its shoulder for one final glance?

One last goodbye?

No more conversations.

I entered Regina's room and looked around to see my mother standing by the bed weeping silently. Dad's head was bowed into his cupped hands, his shoulders shaking slightly as he sobbed. Olen stood over by the window, tears flowing freely. Everyone seemed to have checked their pride at the door. Some sat and looked blankly at the wall, while others comforted the ones next to them. But they all had tear-stained faces and sorrow holding them hostage.

It was May when, in the spirit, Regina climbed the ladder...

...she climbed it to the very top.

Chapter Fourteen

LETTING GO

Back home from the hospital and all too soon, we planned my sister's funeral. As was traditional, the Amish have the viewing and the funeral in their homes. Since we would have more room in the collar shop, we decided to have the service there.

But the visitation hours would be held in the house.

The hearse arrived with the casket, and Dad met the driver and directed him up into one of the bedrooms where Regina's casket was placed.

People from the neighborhood were called and soon arrived to help with all the work. Young men came to care for the chores and milking, and ladies prepared food and took care of the house duties.

The family sat in the upstairs living room when people started to arrive. Buggies, cars, and van loads with well-wishers came in what seemed like an endless stream.

There were family, friends, neighbors that traveled from across the community and other distant Amish communities to show their support, sympathy, and respect for Regina and our family.

The line of visitors continued for hours, moving slowly as people shook hands with each one of us. They followed the line to the bedroom to view Regina's body, sign the guestbook, and then some of them sat down for a while. Others filed back outside and left.

The final day of visitation came, which was the day for the funeral. There was a surprise downpour as hundreds of people showed up for the services. The work benches, sewing machines, and the lacing table where I stood lacing the leather rawhide into collars had been cleaned and carefully prepped for company.

Flashbacks of Regina and I standing there at the table haunted me as the three-hour funeral commenced with a song followed by Scripture reading.

There was a main message, then the closing with some more singing. It seemed like the service dragged on forever, but I found myself hoping time would just stand still. I knew what this was all building up to.

This was the day when my family would all gather around a box that held the remains of my beloved sister—the final cradle and casket.

One last look at that face.

Each expressing their emotions in their own way. Some would sob loudly, while others just silently shook with grief. There were those who could only steal a quick glance then turn away.

My day dreaming of her was interrupted by the congregation shuffling their feet following the last prayer. It was time for our family to walk up and stand around the casket for the last time.

I don't recall that much about what each of my siblings did, but I can still see my mother and father, both tired and emotionally drained. They stood there and wept quietly.

Undoubtedly, they recalled the day she was born, the day she spoke her first word and took her first step. The day the hem of her dress was set ablaze by her two older brothers, Marlin and Ken, who decided they needed to know exactly how matches worked. She was fourteen months old.

Even as she lay in the casket, I could see the scar.

The morning Mom packed her lunch box and watched as she proudly strolled off with her siblings to her first day of school. The rocky stages of adolescence and the trying times of latter teen years.

But through it all, they loved her and would have given anything for her safety and happiness. They probably were aware this day may come, and perhaps even tried to prepare themselves for it. But nothing could prime them for the finality of death and separation from their child.

It goes against everything in a parents being.

After some time, one by one the family started to step away from the casket. This was the signal to the funeral director that the service was at an end.

It had arrived... what I was dreading the most.

Letting go.

The funeral director respectfully stepped forward and without a sound, closed the lid to the casket as if sealing in a part of my past and future. As the lid lowered, I caught one final glimpse of her face.

Then, it was done.

I would never hear her voice again; never...

Our days of milking cows together were over. The times of her and I sitting on the couch with our favorite songbook as she lovingly flipped through the pages and sang a verse or two of every song she recognized. I knew I would truly miss coming into the house and being met by the smell of her freshly baked cinnamon rolls or cookies.

There was only one more thing left to do before this dreadful day would be over—the trip to the gravesite.

Like train cars, the long line of buggies methodically winded through the neighborhood to the nearby community Amish graveyard.

I watched as the casket was lowered into that bottomless hole in the ground. The pallbearers, four of Regina's school classmates, scattered shovels full of dirt down onto the wooden surface. The breeze blew gently, interrupted only by an occasional sniffle, cough, and the shovels as they dug into the dirt again and again.

Like the books she used to read to me, Regina's story had come to an end....a beautiful 22-year-old tale of compassion and grace.

Twenty-two years...

seven months...

and fourteen days.

Chapter Fifteen

REGINA'S PRAYER

As time went on, Ken's reality settled in.

How long does it take for something so drastic to become normal? Would it ever be normal?

Dick Ohnstadt was a friend of our family that lived in Moses Lake, Washington, and he knew of a doctor in Anchorage, Alaska that he insisted my brother go see. And after much debate, the decision was made that Ken and Marianna would make the trip to Washington.

Dick was eager to make the necessary arrangements for them to board a Ferry that would take them from Washington to Anchorage, but one question remained: How were we going to get there?

Since Amish don't generally fly except for emergencies, and it would be much too far to travel in a passenger van, we decided to go in a Class C RV with my cousin Marvin doing the driving.

Wow, a real motorhome!

Well, it was actually a large van with some RV features like a restroom, kitchen, and a bedroom. The kitchen and restroom were barely in working order, but it didn't dull my enthusiasm the least bit.

We were going on a trip—a big one!

I don't remember what the method was for choosing the lucky contestants—those who would actually get to go—but along with Ken, Marianna and their two children, it was my brother Olen and his new bride Bertha, my sister LeAnna, and I that would make up the crew that would embark on this trip to the west coast.

The trip would take two weeks, and we would have the opportunity to see the Pacific Ocean! Over 2,100 miles from our home in Montgomery Indiana. The mere thought was too amazing to believe.

The RV was old with a lot of miles on it, and it had been in storage for a long time. Needless to say, its ability was questionable. For added safety, we tied a horseshoe onto the rear axle. The myth was, that if you hang it so that it dangles there upside down, it will pour away all bad luck from your road trip.

Ironically, I think we blew out and replaced all six of its tires on the way to Washington, and ended up in the shop with mechanical problems at least once.

So much for myths and luck.

We were unanimously relieved when we arrived at Dick's house. He and his wife Jodi welcomed us with a hospitality that certainly was an oasis for the weary travelers from Indiana, and I recall sleeping very well that night.

We awoke the next morning to the sound of Jodi bustling around in the kitchen making breakfast for all of us. Since she was used to cooking for two, having nine additional guests to feed took a lot of extra work.

Dick expanded the table and gathered additional chairs from various rooms of the house.

"Be careful everyone, it's hot!" Jodi said as she carried a huge pot of steaming oatmeal and set it down in front of us.

With all the activity, no one noticed who was missing. Dick knocked lightly on Ken and Marianna's bedroom door.

"Kenneth is very sick," Marianna said wearily through the slightly opened door.

His sky-rocketing fever and sweating were constant for the next four days as he battled a raging kidney infection. It was obvious that he wouldn't be able to make the appointment with the doctor in Alaska.

Dick flipped into rescue mode, unwilling to accept that our entire trip might end up being pointless. After several carefully placed calls, Dick managed to convince the doctor to fly into Seattle and meet Ken there.

A few days later, Ken seemed to have conquered the infection, though weak and tired. And since the doctor didn't have an office in in Seattle, they agreed to meet at a hotel.

When they arrived in the room, the physician was already there studying the X-rays that had been sent to him a few weeks earlier.

He was about six feet tall, had a respectable size mustache, and a kind smile. He pointed out several things he had noticed in the images, one being Ken's spinal cord had not been severed.

"Mr. Raber," he said softly, "after thoroughly examining these X-rays, I see no medical reason why you can't walk."

This wasn't the first time Ken had heard this but hearing it again from a doctor of this stature brought a new wave of optimism. There was a spark in Ken's eyes again. And although the wheelchair he rested in refused to let him escape reality for very long, the words of that doctor begged the question...

...did he dare believe there was real hope?

Ken was twenty-six years old with a wife and two adorable little children. The thought of never being able to run and play ball with his little boy, or hold the hand of his little princess on a daddy-daughter walk was excruciating.

He would choose to hold on to all he had—hope, faith, and the doc's words.

Two weeks went by faster than we thought possible, and suddenly it was time to make the long trek back to Indiana. We enjoyed our final meal from Jodi's kitchen before the packing began.

We waved goodbye to our dear friends in Washington as we drove out of the driveway, and watched as Dick, Jodi, and their little house disappeared in the distance.

We were headed home.

† † †

After losing Regina to cancer, I wish I could say that my next ten years got better, but that isn't true. I made a lot of bad choices and, without a doubt, repeatedly broke my parents' hearts.

Just like many of my peers, my teen life was filled with immorality, tobacco, liquor, and shattered relationships. I lived for the weekend, sinking lower and lower into the pit I already knew was full of hopelessness. I knew my parents were grieved by my selfish behavior, but I chose to ignore them again and again.

My conscience became callused as I hardened against the still, small voice I heard within me. I was bound and determined to find something that would bring relief to the destitution that raged in my soul—a journey that started with seemingly harmless things, but now suddenly grew into something that even I was frightened by.

Friday nights were the beginning of what were always highly anticipated weekends. I would help with the chores and wrap up a few details before getting dressed to leave. As I headed out the door, as usual, my father's concern was all too evident. He would begin to try and reason with me about what I was doing.

The dreaded and predictable "talks"—words of disrespect and suspicion were exchanged, and I repeatedly and angrily rejected his wisdom. It always ended the same way with me walking away, even slamming the door in his face.

The second that door shut with me on one side and my dad on the other, I was overcome with regret. I knew I had made a terrible mistake. Even though I was living like I was bulletproof, on the inside I was filled with anger, bitterness, and fear. I felt like I needed to drown the emotions out before they got the best of me. But the endless attempts to fill the void with alcohol, partying, and failed relationships were a sorry excuse for happiness and fulfillment.

The cycle seemed hopeless and never ending.

I relentlessly pushed through random affairs, irregular behavior, self-indulgence, and many other things to get rid of the ugliness. But no matter how I tried, I failed repeatedly to find relief.

There just didn't seem to be an answer.

I needed something more; something besides all the things that clearly were not working. Though many of my friends regularly used drugs, up to this point, I couldn't bring myself to try it. My sister Regina had suffered and wilted away right before my eyes, and I couldn't imagine getting addicted to something that would slowly kill me from the inside out. I shuddered at the thought of looking in the mirror one day and realizing that I too was dying, by choice, not cancer.

She had warned me repeatedly to stay away from drugs and the people that used them, and so far I had been successful. But I wasn't sure if I could do it much longer. And now with her gone, I was starting to warm up to the idea.

One night while driving around alone struggling with a relationship,

I decided this would be the night. I would do it.

I arrived at the party, tied my horse Star to the hitching post, then walked toward the noisy crowd. In the midst of everyone in that tightly packed shed, the loud music and the occasional falling drunk, my eyes scanned for someone I thought could supply me with what I wanted. But my effort was futile.

It was no use... I decided to go home.

But instead of making my way back to the one secure place where people loved and cared about me, I made a call to a friend. One I knew normally had some heroin.

Aware of my commitment to abstain from drugs, he actually supported me in it. So, it was with great delight that he told me his supply was dry. He didn't have any. I felt a mixture of disappointment, relief, and shame.

The ride home was lonely; only the crunching of my wheels on the gravel and the steady clip-clop of Star's hooves to keep me company.

I felt so stupid... what had I just done!

My heart raced as I realized how close I'd come to doing something so ludicrous. What was wrong with me? Why was I so restless? I had a good family, I was raised going to church, and I had a passion in music. What would drive me to such extreme measures?

By the time I got home, I was grateful that I was spared from my own foolishness, but wasn't entirely certain that conviction to abstain had just been strengthened.

A few months later, the opportunity arose again.

A friend and I were visiting another community. We were just hanging out with some of his cronies when one of them chimed in.

"Let's go back to the house and have some real fun." It's where he had plenty of marijuana.

My friend looked at me as if he expected me to resist the idea, but

I surprised him.

"That's great," I said.

The feeling was even stronger than the time before. Heroin was hardcore, but this could be exactly what I was looking for. Perhaps marijuana would be less risky to my health and could still give me the escape I'd been looking for.

I argued with my conscience and found a false sense of justification in my reasoning.

When we turned off the highway onto a county road, we traveled a few miles then curved into a driveway. There was a big red barn on the right, and we circled around to finally stop in the front of the huge white house.

It was nearly midnight.

Everyone else was relaxed and jabbered in small talk, but I was stiff with anxiety. Still, it didn't matter. This was the moment and I was planning to go through with it no matter what.

We went into the house and sat down at the kitchen table. After a few minutes, our host entered wearing a smile and holding a metal container. He set it on the table, inviting my friend to crack open the box and light up. I suddenly felt uneasy as I watched him lift the lid, then paused.

"It's empty!" he laughed.

"What?" our host responded. "That's impossible! I just filled it before I left tonight."

Everyone seemed perturbed but me. I was in a daze, mesmerized by this unique mystery.

I couldn't help but think I had just been saved from my own stupidity by the mighty hand of God.

Perhaps someone's prayers were just answered.

Maybe Regina's.

PLAIN LESSON FOR LIFE

Religion—the Enemy of God

Many of us that grew up going to church feel or have felt a real desire to be a good person and please God.

Imagine with me that a farmer was visited by a traveling salesman who claimed to have the finest apple tree seeds around. The farmer was quickly persuaded it was true, and soon he held a bag of the impressive seeds. He smiled and waved at the salesman as he drove away.

In due time, the farmer witnessed the first fruit of his amazing tree, but can't believe its dangling fruit—oranges!

Meanwhile, the farmer had been bragging to his neighbors for months about his new apple tree that would bear apples like no other. In a determined panic, he made a sign in big letters painting the words "Apple Tree" on it.

Fastening the sign to a stake, he pounded it into the ground at the base of the tree, satisfied that its proclamation would make it true.

To his utter dismay, the next morning he found the tree still had oranges hanging from it. Unwilling to give up, after dusk, he slipped out to his orchard, grabbed some buckets and began plucking the oranges as fast as he could.

Exhausted, he heaved ten buckets of the unwanted fruit into the back of his truck and sped down the road to get rid of the evidence.

He slept well that night.

A few days later, he went out to see his tree, but again, oranges dangled unashamedly from its branches. The farmer was now livid. He tried one final time to deny the fruit from his uncompromising tree, draping a huge tarp over it so that no one could see the unwanted fruit.

"Now, with a little positive thinking, this stubborn tree will see it my way."

We all know this story is silly. No matter what the farmer tries, his orange tree can never be an apple tree. Its DNA causes it to bear the fruit it was designed to produce.

As crazy as it sounds, sometimes we as church people do the same thing. We set out to be good people, but are often disturbed by the fruit we see coming from our lives. We may make bold statements about who we are in spite of the obvious fruit.

Frustrated and tired of trying to change ourselves, we resort to the last straw. We'll hide the unwanted fruit and think positive thoughts in hopes to dispel what we fear most—that we aren't as blameless as we would like to be.

"For the mind that is set on the flesh is hostile to God, for it does not submit to God's law; indeed, it cannot. Those who are in the flesh cannot please God" (Romans 8:7-8).

We have a problem. A deep-seated problem. Jesus taught that the issue was within our hearts, a sin nature that we inherited from our first father, Adam. And no matter how hard we try, we can never change the outcome.

When this reality hits us, the sound of the gospel—the good news—is like balm to our sin sickened souls! Unlike the orange tree, there is actually hope for us!

When questioned by a Jewish ruler named Nicodemus, Jesus answered, "Truly, truly, I say to you, unless one is born of water and the Spirit, he cannot enter the kingdom of God. That which is born of the flesh is flesh, and that which is born of the Spirit is spirit" (John 3:5-6 ESV).

Points to ponder as you consider growing in the true fruit of the Spirit:

- The power of sin is in its secrecy
- Like the farmer, the only thing religion can offer is a try harder mentality
- The new birth Jesus spoke about offers us a new nature
- What religion can never offer, Jesus gives freely—life—a total change of our DNA

"Therefore, if anyone is in Christ, he is a new creation. The old has passed away; behold, the new has come" (II Corinthians 5:17).

"The thief comes only to steal and kill and destroy. I came that they may have life and have it abundantly" (John 10:10 ESV).

Chapter Sixteen

WHO IS GOD?

The next few years proved to be a cycle of ups and downs. The glamor and excitement of parties and loose living began to lose its significance, and my thoughts returned to when I was fifteen and searching for God.

Who was God? That seemed to be a question this Amish boy should never have to ask since I grew up going to church and hearing stories preached from the Bible. Nonetheless, it persisted.

Who is God?

The biggest drive behind that battle was my fear of death. I was hoping that the alcohol and crazy living would dull that dread.

It was time to find the real answer.

But where would I start? I was so confused. I knew there were so many different opinions about who God was, but who was right? Which view would I—should I—embrace?

My parents and their parents for generations had been faithful to the Amish way of life. Was God Amish? Do Amish have special favor in Gods eyes? At a younger age, I assumed that in the beginning, all people were Amish then slowly started leaving the faith, and we were now among the few that remained.

I was certain it was the root cause for all the sin and pain on the earth. I loved the Amish lifestyle, but of course, I daydreamed of what it would be like to wear store bought clothes and drive a car. I also deeply cherished the quietness and simplicity of my Amish community. I always pictured myself following in the footsteps of my fathers, marrying an Amish girl with a similar worldview, settling down in the community on a few acres with a house and a barn, and work for my dad in the leather business. Possibly even eventually taking over for him.

One of the bright spots in my life was the little acapella singing group I was invited to join. We sang for the elderly and for an endless amount of Mennonite weddings. I was finding more joy and fulfillment in that than I was in the party life.

As I meditated on the simpler things, the noise in my head started to die down a bit, and suddenly for the first time, I began to notice the actual lyrics of songs. I found solace in singing them. The melodies were filled with Biblical principles and stories, and talked about God and His Love.

The others in my group periodically discussed their meaning, and suddenly, I realized that some of the answers to my questions about God were right in those very songs—the phrases I had been singing since childhood.

It changed my life!

But with this revelation came two new challenges. When we sang in the Mennonite weddings, we normally gathered around a microphone so the congregation could hear us. This was a problem since it was a direct violation to the Amish church standards at that time.

I was even visited and encouraged by our Amish ministers to stop breaking the rule. But the singing helped me escape the darkness of my previous lifestyle that grieved everyone, including me. I considered it a real step of progress. Nonetheless, it remained a concern to the church.

Then it dawned on me: Why was it so important to be Amish? Did God care whether or not I was or I wasn't? Did God even see different denominations?

I kept digging for the answers and started entertaining the unprecedented thought of possibly not being Amish.

With this new mindset, people around me started getting frustrated. Some had good answers that helped me understand things, but others told me to simply bloom where I was planted.

In other words, embrace the Amish lifestyle.

As I sat with Mom and Dad to seek their council, they also advised me to join the Amish church and settle down. But Amish or not Amish, one thing I knew for certain, I wanted to obey God and honor my parents.

With that commitment, I began the instruction class for joining the church to become a member. The decision brought a great amount of comfort and security—I would be a good Amish person and feel accepted by the whole community.

What a relief!

I went out, got a haircut, and declared war on my ill habits—smoking, drinking, partying, and even the audio stereo system in my buggy would have to go. If I was going to be Amish, I was going to give it my best shot.

I sold my buggy and bought one more acceptable to the church with no stereo, no tinted windows, and less reflector tape on the wheels. I was really off and running.

Now I could drive into church and not feel guilty, and I had no fear of being approached by the ministers with regard to my behavior or my ride. My buggy was clean, empty, and even smelled fresh! The comfort of being accepted was overwhelming.

I discovered that my favorite preachers from childhood hadn't changed; I still loved to hear them preach as much as when I was a boy. I basked in their messages and stories, especially when they mixed a lot of English in with their German.

But to my surprise, my course didn't put an end to my questions. I kept asking, "Who is God?" and it was still being driven by my intense fear of death.

I bought a new Parallel Bible with German on one side and the King James Version on the other. I threw myself into reading it starting in the Gospels, but unfortunately that only created more questions for me to wrestle with.

What was sin? Who decided what sin was? What did it mean to forgive? How did God view gossip? What was the meaning of John 3:16? Why did we sing "Amazing Grace, how sweet the sound that saved a wretch like me" when we didn't believe in being saved? Why do some people say you must be born again? Born again, what is that?

I started comparing the Bible and the life of Jesus to the reality of my life and what I found was disturbing. Some friends told me I should stop reading the Bible or thinking about it so much.

"Come on, man," they said, "just be your old self again and party with us. Forget about this stuff."

But the thought of that made me sick. I was completely done trying to drown out my questions with partying. Going back was not an option!

Other Amish friends encouraged me to keep searching for answers as my frustration began to build. I recognized it and deeply hated what was happening.

Why can't I just be normal?

I knew how leaving the Amish church would devastate my family. I was repeatedly assured that one doesn't have to be Amish to go to Heaven, but if you are born Amish, it is best to stay Amish.

I decided to finish the course I had started in order to be baptized. I was the new Amos—the one that was well behaved and accepted. I could sense the appreciation for the one that now went to the youth singings instead of the parties, and that wasn't hard since I loved singing anyway.

Mid-week and Sunday evenings found me going to volleyball games and singing services held at one of the youth's parents' house. I felt liberated. Instead of going to the local convenient store for my weekend stash of beer and cigarettes, I played the harmonica to the rhythm of Stars hooves as they clip-clopped on our way across the countryside.

Then the day came—it was Baptism Sunday.

The church service was held at our neighbor's home, and the line of youth that completed the class entered behind the ministers, single file.

It was the anticipated moment, and adrenaline was pumping. The service started with the normal routine of singing, scripture reading, then the main message began. After a few hours, the service was almost over when Bishop Ben stood.

"If it's still your will to be baptized, please kneel."

Without a verbal response, feet shuffled as the whole line of young people dropped from the bench onto their knees. Bishop Ben summoned one of the other ministers to come, and they began.

Finally, they reached me. The assisting minster cupped his hands over my head to create a funnel for the water, and Bishop Ben made three precise pours as he reckoned.

"I baptize you in name of the Father, the Son and the Holy Ghost into the church of Jesus Christ. Do you promise to be an up-building member of the church of Christ as long as you live?"

"Yes," I replied without hesitation.

He then extended the right hand of fellowship and greeted me with the holy kiss. In most Amish communities, that is the apex of becoming a dedicated Amish person, and is believed to be the way to be born again.

I tried to calm myself enough to discern whether or not I felt any different. And if I wasn't feeling different then, I was sure that it would come later. We sang the last song before Ben announced where the services would be held in two weeks. Then we were all dismissed. I left the house and started my walk home.

I did it… I finished the course. I was baptized and now a member of the Old Order Amish Church of Daviess County Indiana.

So why did I feel discouraged.

I stayed on course for several months, but to my shame and regret, I could feel myself sliding right back into the dark grip of my previous habits and strongholds. I remember the night I asked one of my friends for a cigarette. Instead of handing one over, he scolded me and said he wasn't willing to enable me to start that bad habit again.

Why am I doing this?

I had successfully stopped smoking and was doing well, but suddenly the urge to have a cigarette was stronger than I was. And though at first my friend wasn't willing to put a nail in my coffin, after several minutes, he ended up giving in.

I walked away from his buggy so I would be alone. For me, smoking was wrong. I knew it. Still, I put that cigarette to my lips and snapped the lighter.

I'm going to enjoy a cigarette.

The little flame flickered then made contact with the tobacco. I drew in a nice big breath.

Auuuh. I waited for the feeling of fulfillment. I waited… and waited…

But it never came. Instead, as the smoke filled my lungs, a stinging sensation grabbed hold of my chest followed by dizziness much like when I first started.

I instantly regretted my decision. I knew that if I was serious about quitting this ruthless habit, I had just taken several steps backwards.

The ride home that night was long and lonely. The clip-clop of Star's hooves only reminded me of the sense of peace I had just a few hours earlier as I traveled to sing. Now, now it was replaced with an unmistakable sense of ruin.

Why was it so hard? If being born again through baptism was the answer, then why did it seem virtually impossible to get victory over these cold chains? I felt like I was in a secret prison of habits.

†††

My downward spiral continued and slowly destroyed what I had built over the past several months. I hated it with everything in me, but it seemed I was out of control. My heart began to sink to the reality.

I had failed.

I was dishonoring my parents, the church, and ultimately God! The sin mounted higher and higher until finally I was right back where I'd started—partying, drinking, and smoking was my normal again. I knew so many of my friends were upset with me, but I pushed ahead, determined to put all these failed attempts behind me. No matter how hard I tried, I just couldn't be good.

After a few months, I began to think that maybe I should leave the Amish church and join a conservative Mennonite congregation. I sought council from several of my friends, and finally sat down with my parents.

I knew they would be disappointed, and they were.

We talked about so much, but there was one piece of wisdom my dad shared that has stayed with me to this day.

"In a fallen world, there is no perfect church. Any congregation made up of people will have issues and struggles. If you can't find your answers in the Amish church, you'll also not find them in the Mennonite church."

Either way, I wasn't ready to believe him. I needed to find out for myself. My next mission was to join the Mennonites. And when I did, it was almost a perfect repeat of my experience in the Amish church.

A perfect failure.

I was still so confused. Had I sinned so badly that I couldn't be forgiven?

What would happen to me when I died?

Who was God?

Lord, please answer me.

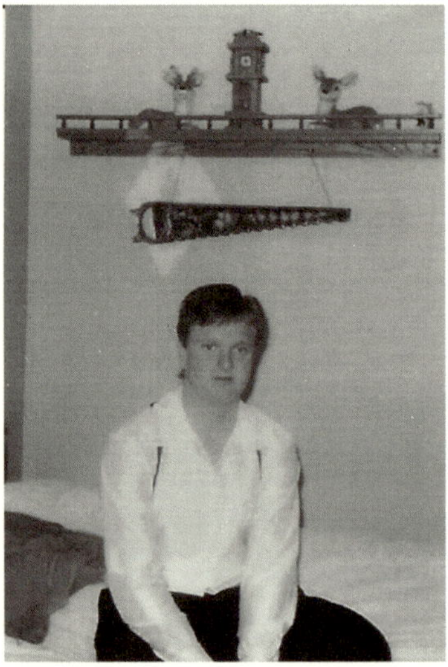

Amos at approximately 19 years old

Chapter Seventeen

A DIVINE ACCIDENT

I was twenty years old when I had secured my commercial driver's license and was driving semi for a local company. Southern Indiana was in coal, and the mines had been in full harvest mode for many years. It was a dirty job, and I often came home with my face covered with black coal dust. But I didn't care since I was living my childhood dream—operating an eighteen wheeler!

A few months later, a friend and I decided to pack everything we owned in a cardboard box and move to Sarasota, Florida. I was making payments on a 1997 Chevy truck and had $1,000 to my name.

Barely out of my teens and living in Florida with no job didn't last very long. We scanned the papers daily and watched for job opportunities, and I eventually landed a part-time position in construction. Not my favorite work, but at least it brought in some cash for miscellaneous spending and money for my truck payment. What little was left over I squandered on the weekend.

Each evening, I went to the famous Pinecraft Park—the large Amish community park that offered a variety of recreational opportunities. It was where everyone went to socialize and see what was happening. Night after night, my friend and I did this with nothing out of the ordinary happening. Volleyball and basketball games, people standing around in huddles talking about all the latest gossip. A random flow of bicycles with people just like me, wanting to see what was going on at the park.

One night, I heard there was going to be a singing group performing called The Gospel Express. I'd never heard of them, but decided to go and check them out.

The parking lot was packed, but I found a place on the street and shut off my truck's engine. As I got out and walked toward the pavilion, I could see the group playing and hear their beautiful singing.

Nestled within the crowd, I listened as the gray-haired guy who seemed to be the leader in the group continually talked about Jesus and the things of God, especially the blood of Jesus Christ. I could tell all of them had a joy and peace that I didn't have—so much so that it actually made me feel uncomfortable.

And I left.

Going to the park was a nightly routine, visiting with people, playing volleyball, and doing whatever else there was to do.

It was in late December when a few of my friends and I were parked on the street at an intersection when suddenly a young, gorgeous blonde lady barely five feet tall on roller skates ran smack into the side of my truck.

It startled me!

I was sure she had to be hurt or, at the very least, my truck had a dent in it. But she smiled sheepishly, apologized, then glided back off into the night, gone just as quickly as she had arrived.

What was that all about?

Who was she and why had I not seen her there before?

Trying to hide my intense curiosity, I attempted to find out her name, but no one seemed to know who she was.

Now she was gone, but she didn't leave my mind for a long time. Her beautiful smile wasn't easy to forget.

Over the next few days, I realized I was obsessed with the stranger on roller skates and our mysterious meeting. From that moment, going to Pinecraft had a new purpose.

† † †

For several days I didn't see her. What was worse, I didn't even know her name! I found myself describing her to people around me as I tried to identify her. It was a true case of Cinderella Syndrome. Some people knew who I was talking about, but they didn't know her name or where she was staying.

Then one night someone told me that her name was Amanda Byler.

Mystery solved!

But the search continued. Night after night I stood in the park and watched for her, passing the time by visiting with people. But my eyes were continually scanning the crowd, at every face, at each newcomer.

At long last, she showed up!

I knew it was her at a glance, though I had only seen her the one time. There was no way I could mistake her sparkling eyes and golden hair.

After watching her for several minutes, I got up the courage to approach her. I introduced myself and she was warm, friendly, and I came to find out that we shared some mutual friends. Her best friend just happened to be my first cousin, Malinda Raber. I couldn't believe it.

She was kind, but her attention soon turned to someone else, and I drifted back into the shadows of the parking lot, my heart racing.

Wow! I finally got to meet her, but I didn't know much more about her than I did before. Who was she, and where was she from? How old was she, and most importantly, was she single?

Over the next few weeks, we crossed paths periodically, and got to know each other on a first name basis. Much to my delight, I never saw anyone with her that would indicate she was married, and soon she gave me her phone number. I really liked her and wanted our friendship to be more than just random park pals.

A dinner date was the next logical step.

Several days later, I worked up the nerve to give her a call. She remembered me and through all of my stuttering and stammering, I asked her out. She said she needed to think about it for a day or two.

She didn't say no!

Nearly sick with anticipation, I tried to occupy myself as I waited for her call. I avoided the park until I heard from her for fear of an awkward encounter.

I waited 24 hours for the phone to ring. And after some appropriate introductory small-talk and asking her one more time if she'd like to have dinner with me, she said yes!

Unbelievable!

I wasted no time. I got my truck all shined up, picked out my best outfit, and prepared for the big date.

It was the first Friday in January when I made myself as spiffy as I knew how, and marched out of the house on my way to pick up Amanda.

Amanda... even her name was beautiful.

I pulled into the driveway a few minutes before our agreed time of 6:30pm.

She answered the door looking absolutely gorgeous, dressed in stone washed jeans and a white embroidered top. I'll never forget the pride I felt as I placed her in the passenger seat.

At the restaurant of her choice, we were seated in a booth where she ordered her favorite, Oriental Chicken Salad with extra dressing, and I ordered a burger and fries. Funny the little things you remember.

I'm sure neither one of us had a big appetite, but our awkwardness quickly disappeared as we discovered that we were comfortable in the other's presence. In what seemed like minutes, our dinner was over and the bill was laying on our table.

As I counted out the cash to pay for the meal, she noticed I hadn't included a tip.

"Do you not tip?" she asked, confused.

"No, not normally," I answered.

Let's just say that from that day on, I've been a faithful tipper. With the right kind of persuasion, it seems that even an old dog can learn new tricks.

We found that we had a lot in common that night as we visited for hours. As time passed and our relationship grew, we confided in each other more and more. It was official...

...we were in love, all due to one small divine accident.

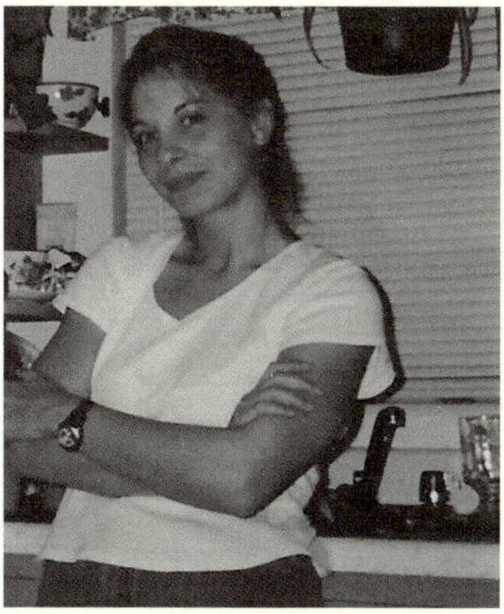

Amanda

Chapter Eighteen

WHEREVER YOU GO

If we could have turned forward the hands of time, if we could have seen the future ahead of us, I'm sure we would have ran in opposite directions. But life happens one day at a time for a reason—the ups and downs and surprises can be exhilarating and also exhausting.

Amanda was self-employed in house cleaning while I had a daytime trucking job, but we both made our schedules work to spend the evenings together. We went on walks and talked for hours late into the night. We shared our hopes and dreams as well as our regrets.

We also spoke honestly about our childhood and shed tears together as we let down our guard. It was really the first time I had ever talked about some of the darker secrets that I held inside—the sexual abuse that I had yet to deal with emotionally, much like her.

Amanda often insisted that I bring my guitar to play some music for her. No doubt, she was my biggest self-appointed fan. She was positive I should move to Nashville and pursue a career in Country

Music. And since my first love was music, time would only tell if I would be persuaded.

Sitting so attentively, Amanda watched and listened as I sang to her, and she would join me when she knew the lyrics. We laughed at the funny songs and cried to some of the sad ones.

Music was our mutual friend.

Amanda had left her home in Michigan years before, and though she maintained some connection with some of her family, due to some previous relational strains, there was still some unrest there. Her family wished it could be different, and so did she.

Her parents spent their winters in Florida and she wanted me to meet them. I was more than a little nervous, but when she insisted, I agreed to go with her.

Upon our arrival, I nervously followed her toward the house. She grabbed my hand and pulled me toward the door, and with that lovely grin assured me that everything would be okay.

"What's not to like?" she said, a rhetorical question she believed could never be answered.

"They're going to love you."

When we entered the house, the kitchen smelled so warm and welcoming, it reminded me of home. We were greeted with the smiling faces of her parents, Jake and Verna Byler. Her brother Ray joined us, as well.

Her dad was a tall Amish man with gray hair and a well-maintained long gray beard. I liked him instantly. Likewise, her mother was friendly, and the chatter flowed as we sat around the table enjoying a meal of fresh-caught Florida fish.

As the meal progressed, I was a witness to the reuniting that took place between Amanda and her parents; the forgiveness that was granted, and the healthy reconciliation that was real. We spent many nights with her family having supper, playing games, and taking long walks. It was like she couldn't get enough, almost like she entered a second childhood and gained a new sense of excitement for life and her future.

Well, with our relationship advancing so quickly, we were starting to talk about our next step. Was Sarasota, Florida where we wanted to live?

Amanda's friend, Malinda, was who she would miss the most. Yes, she loved her house cleaning clients and served them with loyalty, but she was willing to leave it all behind if I wanted to move north—somewhere closer to Indiana and Michigan, our home states.

It was all so perfect. Wherever she wanted to go, that's where I wanted to be.

† † †

In late April, I received a job offer from a business located in Goshen, Indiana. Trucking was what I really wanted to do, and this job sounded promising. We decided to pack up and move there to embark on a brand new life together.

One by one, she informed all her friends and clients of her decision to move north—a decision that was met with resistance, but nothing like her friend Malinda.

"What do you think you're doing, Missy?!" she scolded Amanda. "We have known each other since we were little girls, and now you're going to up and leave me and run off with my cousin?"

"I love him. He's the one, and I'll go wherever he goes," she replied calmly.

"What?" Malinda couldn't believe what she was hearing. "You hardly know him! How can you possibly know you love him or even trust him?"

But Amanda wouldn't budge. "There's just something about him. From our first dinner date, I knew I could trust him. Now, I've grown in love with him, and that's not going to change."

And that was the final word on that. Like I said, Amanda could be very persuasive.

For the move, we rented a U-Haul trailer, loaded all of our belongings into it, hitched it to the back of my truck, and headed north.

In all honestly, I couldn't believe Amanda would do it—leave so many years of memories behind her.

But she did.... for me.

She was sold out to our new life together, and her commitment to our relationship was overwhelming. It confirmed deep within me what I had already suspected—I truly loved this girl and wanted to spend the rest of my days with her.

She needed a pet name. But what could I call such an angel? The answer seemed obvious.

I would call her "Sweets."

† † †

After a brief stop in Daviess County to see my parents, Amanda and I traveled on to Northern Indiana. When we arrived, it was a cool, dreary day in April. The rain and sleet was intermittent but persistent for the next several days.

Do they ever have a nice day here? I wondered.

Through connections of friends, we had arranged for lodging. Millersburg, Indiana was our new home, at least for now.

The first day weather permitted, I made a trip to the trucking company that was hiring—the whole reason we moved. I was met with bad news: They had filled their positions and didn't need any more drivers.

What? I moved from Florida for that job!

How could there not be any available? Since Amanda was experienced in house cleaning, she quickly picked up a job in Middlebury while I watched for opportunities, made phone calls, and visited businesses to no avail.

As the search continued, I occasionally landed some part-time work, but nothing long lasting. Then through a friend, I found out about a job opening just a few miles from where I lived. Wasting no time, I arrived at the office, introduced myself, and after some small-talk, the manager hired me on the spot.

I just landed a job and would be starting the following week. It was time to celebrate!

I guess wherever you go, together, is home.

Amanda and Amos

Chapter Nineteen

GOD IS EVERYWHERE

Li'l Digger Transport in Millersburg...it even sounded like my kind of place. My new assignment as a semi-truck driver would be hauling lumber into the RV factories and forty thousand pound steel coils in and out of Chicago. It would force me to drive at levels I wasn't prepared for. I was familiar with making my way through small towns, but I wasn't mentally ready for urban areas of Chi Town. But after a few short months, it became a daily routine.

Amanda heard about a job opportunity at R&R Woodworking in Nappanee, and decided straight away to leave house cleaning to try something new—and she loved it!

She also enjoyed going with me when I had a weekend run to make. Our most memorable time was to Jonesville, Wisconsin. On that trip, we wrote a song together that we titled, "Midnight Hour"—just another "love gone bad" country song, but it was ours.

Though we faced the usual challenges that dating couples face, sometimes we weren't sure we were going to be able to work them out. But somehow, we always did.

We wanted to find a church to be a part of, but where do you start in an area as big as Northern Indiana? In a community that size, there were lots of church options. We didn't know many people, but I remembered I had some relatives living in Nappanee, Glen, and Marge Wagler.

After I made contact with them, they invited us to visit their congregation. Two weekends in a row, we made the forty-minute trip from Millersburg to Nappanee to visit their church, only to drive right past it and go back home.

On the third weekend, we parked, went inside, and sat in the back pew with the intention of leaving right after that last amen. But we couldn't manage it thanks to the friendly people there who reached out to us, welcomed us, and thanked us for coming.

Honestly, it made me a bit uncomfortable, and I vowed never to step through those doors again.

For some weird reason, we were back the following Sunday! And again, the folks welcomed us and made us feel right at home. We didn't know it yet, but we were hooked by the hospitality and kindness this little congregation showed us. They took us in as strangers, but soon enough, we felt like family. I'm ever grateful that they showed us the genuine love of Christ.

After attending for several weeks, we decided to ask for membership. This is where we could have been so easily missed. We were expecting a process of questions, classes, and possibly a time of proving ourselves followed by a special service where it would be announced that Amos and Amanda were now members of Fairview Mennonite Church.

We were totally wrong.

Instead of jumping through the usual hoops of membership, Pastor Loren Graber invited us to his house for grilled steak on the following

Monday evening. I wasn't really sure that a steak dinner was necessary, but we went just the same.

We had a nice evening together with Loren and his wife Esther, but I kept wondering when we were going to talk about our membership. But the night wore on.

Later, when we were all sitting at their kitchen island on bar stools, Pastor Loren leaned over to me and said, "So, you want to become members at our church?"

"Yes," I replied.

He was a short, stocky guy, and I'm more on the tall side. Then he leaned into me and asked a million-dollar question.

"Are you born again?"

I had heard our preachers say the German term *Sie müssen von neuem geboren werden,* which translates as "You must be born again." I was familiar with the term, but not sure what it meant in this context. Recalling that night, I guess I had baptism and being born again wrapped into one package.

I replied, "Yes, I have been baptized."

"That's not what I asked you," he smiled.

Opening his Bible, he took me to Romans, chapter 10, verses 9 and 10.

"That if thou shalt confess with thy mouth the Lord Jesus, and shalt believe in thine heart that God hath raised him from the dead, thou shalt be saved. For with the heart man believeth unto righteousness; and with the mouth confession is made unto salvation."

He explained that the "new birth" was an act of repentance of sin and trusting God to save my soul, and give me new life in my spirit.

I was dumbfounded.

The pastor just looked at me. "Amos, if you went out of here tonight and had an accident and were killed, your soul would spend eternity in hell."

Now, I was completely stunned.

He went on to explain that being baptized was an act of obedience, but it had to come *after* the new birth. Baptism is important, but *it is not* salvation.

"If it was, Jesus wouldn't have needed to die. Jesus didn't leave his home in Heaven, come to earth, live and walk as a man, spend three years in ministry, go through all the agony of rejection by his disciples, receive beatings from the religious crowds and Roman soldiers, and die on a cruel Roman cross just to tell us that in order to be saved we need to be baptized with water by a church leader."

He continued, "As a matter of fact, in Acts chapter 2, when the apostle Peter was preaching to the religious people, they felt the weight of their sin and asked, 'Men and brothers, what shall we do?'

Peter told them they needed to repent and be baptized in the name of Jesus Christ for the forgiveness of sins. They also would receive the Holy Spirit."

Then Pastor Loren turned to the Gospel of John and read where Jesus explained to Thomas that He was the Way, the Truth, and the Life, and that no man comes to the Heavenly Father but through Him.

"Amos," Loren said, "God desires a relationship with you through Jesus Christ. The only thing you need to do is repent, turn away from your life of sin, believe, and follow Him."

He then leaned back in his chair, giving me time to think.

Everything seemed to stop with this new reality. I tried not to show it, but I was deeply troubled. Was this the answer I'd been searching for? Was it always there as the questions harassed me for the past decade?

As Amanda and I left, the pastor and his wife gave us a box of recordings from a tent revival preacher that had recently preached in the area.

Conversation was scarce on the way home that night. Amanda and I had talked about a lot of things, but not so much about God. I'm not sure why it made me squirm, but it did. We arrived at her house, said our goodbyes, and I headed on to my house.

The next morning before leaving for work, I grabbed the box of cassettes.

I guess it couldn't hurt to listen.

Driving a 1996 Model FLD Freightliner with a condo sleeper, I settled in. It was old and tired with over one million miles on it, and several things didn't work, including the AC and the radio. I brought my portable cassette player with me, so I began to listen to the preaching on the tapes.

The truck was so loud, I couldn't hear the player from the passenger seat, so I balanced one end of the player on my shoulder and the other on the back of the seat.

But there was another problem. Since I was a heavy smoker, I couldn't go very long without taking a cigarette break. I'd pause the preaching for a few minutes, quickly get my nicotine fix, and then get back to listening.

The preacher reminded me of some of my favorite Amish preachers, speaking straight from his heart. It was all very real for him.

I was often wiping tears away as I drove listening to him share stories of difficulty, of faith, and of how God took seemingly hopeless situations and redeemed them completely. My crying could turn to laughter in a flash as he told tales that pointed to God's faithfulness through comical circumstances.

His voice sounded vaguely familiar.

Who was this guy?

† † †

After I returned from my trip and saw Pastor Loren again, I asked him. He called to his wife who was in the living room and said, "Esther, don't we have a picture of Nelson somewhere?"

"Here," she replied as she walked toward him holding out a picture.

"What?" I exclaimed. I couldn't believe my eyes. "Wait a minute..." I said hesitantly. I had also heard this voice in my early teen years, but where? Then it all came crashing like a tidal wave.

My semi truck driving friend from childhood—the one I went on the trip with and listened to the recording in the cab of a man preaching and talking about the goodness of God. Then I recalled the gospel group that played in Sarasota, Florida with a white-haired man who talked about Jesus.

It was too wild to be true...

The recordings were of the same man! Nelson Colblentz from Gospel Express Ministries.

Oh, how the Lord works—He's in all places at all times. Nappanee, Sarasota, everywhere.

By this time, I had given some of the cassettes to Amanda. She listened to some of them, then wanted the entire box.

"Oh, no Sweets," I said. "Not a chance. You can have them when I'm done."

We had to come up with a plan that would work for both of us. I gave her half of the recordings, and I kept half. When we were finished listening to our allotment, we would swap. Most of the messages were about an hour long, which was perfect for her since she had a thirty minute drive to work. She listened to the first half on the way to work and the other half on the way home.

Needless to say, the messages stirred up lots of things. We weren't sure what to do with it all. We began to understand that God wanted to bring healing and forgiveness to all the shame, guilt, and anger we had hidden in our lives. The thought of going to counseling and talking about the abuse we had experienced was a little terrifying. Why would we talk about it, especially to total strangers? Ever since it happened, we had been trying to forget it.

We decided that it just wasn't for us and that we should just carry on the way we were and not make any sudden changes. But as we kept listening to the cassettes...

God was there.

He's everywhere.

Chapter Twenty

BLINDSIDED BY THE LIGHT

There was something special about that little country church and the people gathered there. We found ourselves somewhere between accepting their care and holding them at arm's length. Our pursuit for a home church felt attainable, but this idea about a personal relationship with God was scary.

It just seemed absurd.

Perhaps this could be the answer to my lifelong quest for who God was/is. Very unlikely, but possible. Though tempted to run away from it all, I stayed and proceeded with extreme caution. I wanted to attend a church, but wasn't about to put up with religious nuts.

The ministry team had agreed to meet with Amanda and me in order to go through some discipleship classes for membership. We made the trip to Wakarusa to meet with the ministry team in one of the minister's homes.

Like always, they greeted us warmly and opened our time together with prayer and began sharing some scripture verses with flowing conversation that followed.

Suddenly, I fell to pieces and began to weep uncontrollably. I remember feeling so ashamed of myself, but no matter how much I tried, the sobbing wouldn't stop. I was so embarrassed. And when they asked me what was wrong, I couldn't explain it.

Because I didn't know.

Then, one of the ministers asked me if I wanted to pray. My heart screamed no, but my head signaled yes. Slowly, I stood to my feet and followed them into a bedroom where they asked me some questions about what was going through my mind, but I still couldn't put my finger on it.

Finally, one of them asked, "Amos, would you like to pray and ask Jesus into your heart?"

I nodded.

We knelt together by the bedside and they led me in a simple prayer of repentance. I wasn't sure what to expect, but when I stood up, I felt so light I was sure I was floating. All the earthly pleasures I had ever experienced couldn't compare to this. The ministers said that the Bible calls it being born again! The darkness of my being had just been invaded by light, heavenly light!

This, this was exactly what I was looking for all along. I had just received what all the "pain killers" could never give me—peace. It had to be the best kept secret in the universe!

Since the fall in the garden of our first father, Adam, all men are born with a sin nature (Eph 2). The nature of wrath is at work in our hearts. We are enemies with God, and because of a sinful nature, we start to rebel against Him almost immediately as children.

Being a certain denomination or religion can't repair that problem. No matter how hard we try or how good we try to be, there is still a sin nature at work in the depths of us. We try hard to make ourselves and others believe that all is well, but at the end of the day, we know the solemn truth—that we need something more.

We need a miracle!

That's what Jesus Christ came to give us, and that's what happened to me that night.

God in Heaven reached down and put His life in my spirit. He gave me a new heart. I was a new creation in Jesus Christ! I didn't understand it all, but one thing I knew, the chains and heaviness were gone!

How could this be?

I strained for so many years to find peace and couldn't. What had just happened?

The ministers graciously explained that no church—Amish, Mennonite, Baptist, Methodist, or any other—could save me from my sinful human nature. That task was only conquerable by Jesus Christ.

"Wherefore, if any man is in Christ, he is a *new creature:* the old things are passed away; behold, they are become new" (2 Cor 5:17 ASV).

When Amanda and I left that night, I threw two packs of cigarettes into the trash as I proclaimed, "I won't need those anymore."

She wasn't sure what to think about this "new creation." She was friendly to the idea, but kept her distance from going there herself.

† † †

As time passed, I was still overwhelmed by this new found faith. The little church rejoiced with us, and the ministers discipled me on a daily basis. I had so many questions, and they patiently walked with me and tried to explain that I was now in a relationship with the God of Heaven through His Son, Jesus Christ.

Since I grew up in church, I knew all the terms they were using, but the relationship concept was something I had somehow missed. They encouraged me to pray, but it seemed daunting.

"It's simple," they said. "You just talk to God as you would talk to one of us."

I grew up hearing prayer; my dad prayed every morning from the prayer book as did the preachers in church on Sunday. These were prayers that were written down by our respected forefathers. That was something I understood, but just praying from the heart... what a concept!

I got quite accustomed to short prayers like those from Peter the apostle when he was walking on the water and started to sink. He simply called out, "Lord help me!" Jesus on the cross cried, "Father, forgive them for they know not what they do!" and, "Into your hands I commit my spirit."

It was Sunday morning, October 6th when Amanda and I were on our way to church. I noticed a heaviness in her, and I knew she was struggling with some inner battles about being a member and the idea of baptism.

"What's wrong, Sweets?" I asked.

Her response was a slight but labored smile. She wasn't ready to talk about it, so we drove in silence. When we arrived, I visited with others until the service began. But where was Amanda?

I scanned the room and eventually realized she had singled out some folks from church to ask them to pray with her.

I fidgeted nervously. Would she do it?

That little church family had been praying aggressively for our salvation, but Amanda had one huge obstacle in the way. She had this overwhelming fear that God would never be able to accept her. Even though we had often talked about how Jesus clearly said, "I did not come for those that are whole, I came for those that are sick and need a doctor" (Mark 2:17).

He had shown mercy and forgiveness for anyone that came and asked for it.

Amanda and I talked frequently about the verse that says, "If anyone comes to me, I will in no wise cast him out" (John 6:37).

My thoughts were interrupted by the sanctuary door opening, and when I turned to see Amanda along with a few others enter, it was obvious. Her face shone and her smile nearly reached around her head.

She had done it! Like billions of people over the centuries, and even me, she had experienced the meaning of John 3:16.

She had personally met the Redeemer.

In simple faith, my girl had bowed to her knees and asked her Creator to forgive her and give her the new birth that Jesus had made possible for all mankind. We were in, both of us. Members of the same family.

God's family!

Oh, the joy and peace we experienced! Now, we could understand and identify with the stories in the Bible. Throughout that book, normal people like us became partakers of the love, grace, and forgiveness of God. They often responded with tremendous joy. Some received their eyesight, the lame walked, the lepers were cleansed, demons were cast out, adulterers forgiven, and some received household salvation!

They all received it the same way —faith followed by thanksgiving and overwhelming joy.

We were ecstatic, and I'm ever grateful to that faithful congregation at Fairview Mennonite! May God reward them richly for loving and caring for two people like us.

Next came the act of the public confession of faith.

†††

Amanda faced westward and symbolically renounced sin and her past, then turned eastward and embraced Jesus Christ and her new life in Him.

It was awesome!

She beamed with new life and purpose. It was like she couldn't stop smiling. For her testimony, she announced, "If for the rest of my life I can help one person find the peace I found in Jesus, it will have been worth it all!"

She had to make a few phone calls to some of her friends and tell them the good news. Especially Malinda, her friend back in Florida.

"Malinda, Amos and I have been attending this church here in Nappanee, and a few days ago I prayed and asked Jesus to forgive me of my sins and to make me a new creature."

Silence...

"Malinda," she said, "I've been born again and baptized. I'm a Christian!"

Still...nothing.

Their catch-up conversation abruptly dropped like a kite on a dying breeze. Awkward. Malinda was totally flabbergasted. But then, sometimes no words speak loudest of all.

† † †

It all finally made sense. I had been looking for peace in all the wrong places, but true peace can't come from any church. True peace can only come from the Prince of Peace Himself, Jesus Christ.

As it is written: "This is the stone which was set at nought of you builders, which is become the head of the corner. Neither is there salvation in any other: for there is none other name under heaven given among men, whereby we must be saved" (Acts 4:7 and 11-12).

Chapter Twenty-One

AN UNFAMILIAR ROAD

No matter how pretty we try to make it, even after we're born again, there are struggles—arguably more so than before. Since we were being piloted by the Holy Spirit, Amanda and I confronted and experienced battles and struggles we had never faced before. Yes, God had given us a new heart, but we still lived in a fallen world.

Suddenly, I Peter 2:11 made sense to us. "Dearly beloved, I beseech you as strangers and pilgrims, abstain from fleshly lusts, which war against the soul."

I was being convicted about things I'd been doing for years without a second thought.

One thing that strengthened us was praying and discussing the Bible together. Amanda and I also became aware that we needed someone to help us unravel all the feelings and things from the past we were dealing with.

Glen and Marge became a vital part of our everyday life, and Marge especially was a tremendous blessing for Amanda. Any extra time she had was normally spent with Marge and her children. They had known each other from years gone by, and loved catching up. Amanda had asked Marge to sew some clothes for her, and wanted to know what she could do in return. Marge told her she could just come and spend time with her, and maybe assist her with some house work. Of course, Amanda was delighted to do so.

Glen and Marge, along with the church family, walked with us patiently guiding us in understanding the scriptures and also teaching us what it meant to be a Christian.

A friend told us about a counseling ministry in Kalamazoo, Michigan that specialized in helping people that had experienced abuse of any kind.

After wrestling with the fear of such an undertaking, with weeks of encouragement from others, we phoned to apply for the sessions.

We made the two-hour trip and entered with lots of skepticism, but soon we realized that these were people just like us. The stories we heard were amazing, and suddenly we didn't feel so alone. Many had similar stories to ours in regards to sexual abuse—verbal, physical, and even rape.

Some had been in the counseling sessions for a long time and were well advanced in finding healing from the pain. Others were fresh like us with lots of tears being shed.

Suddenly, our problems seemed smaller.

We were all there from a variety of backgrounds, but were all seeking the same thing—healing, forgiveness, and a guilt-free life at peace with God.

Amanda and I made the trip twice a week for the whole term, and when we completed the course, we felt as if a hurricane had hit our lives. Yes, we were well on our way of learning how to deal with our past issues, but somehow, things at that time seemed worse. Like it would be better if we would have never brought it up.

The nest had been stirred and the bees were loose.

†††

My mind goes back to an experience with my horse, Star. We got her as a grown mare, and didn't really know much about her. But we soon found out she had a really bad habit. While tied in the barn, if you walked in front of her she would go into a fit and franticly pull back on her rope and halter.

On one occasion, I recall the look of terror that raged in her eyes. As a young lad, I thought this was just some stupid act she did and needed to be broken from. I was determined to train her to respond differently.

So when she tore back, I would wave my arms and yell at her to try to get her to stop. But no matter how much or how often I did this, it never seemed to help at all.

Today, I would be willing to bet that somewhere in Star's history there was an angry master who beat her on the head or nose. Although we weren't the ones who did it, Star had a terrible fear that it would happen again.

Anytime someone got close to her head, she would respond from memory. What she needed was a master who would speak gently to her and softly rub her head, showing her that he wasn't going to hurt her. In doing so, over time, her trust would be gained.

If I had only known then what I know now, Star would have most likely stopped the learned behavior and recovered emotionally.

This insight comes from a former pastor—now a full-time counselor—and some professional horse trainers who deal with horses similar to

Star on a regular basis. I've witnessed firsthand some of the horses and the changes made after the trainers gain their trust.

The horses inevitably lost their fear.

†††

There was good and bad that came out of the counseling sessions. As Amanda and I sat in the circle of people who had similar experiences, we found it easy to be totally honest with others, and most importantly, with ourselves.

Both of us realized that we had subconsciously tried to minimize the offenses and the pain the abusers caused us. Again, it's very typical for victims to take this route of thinking. It sounds humble and holy to try to minimize the pain that we get from any act of abuse, but in reality, it prolongs our healing and victory.

Think about it. Does ignoring a past violation or convincing ourselves that it wasn't that bad help the situation? We need to take a long, hard look at not only the wound and offense, but also our response.

It makes perfect sense. If Star had the ability to speak, she may have tried to convince me that everything was fine, but her predictable actions told another story.

As Amanda and I continued to recognize the abuse and the pain it brought us, we began to see how predictable our actions were based on what we had experienced. We became painfully aware of how broken we were. But all was not lost. You see, we serve an awesome Redeemer.

"Come unto me, all ye that labor and are heavy laden, and I will give you rest" (Matthew 11:28).

This level of awareness brought me and Amanda to the peak of our life and our relationship, and to a moment that would define the rest of our lives together.

We came home from Kalamazoo late one night, and our hearts were heavy—even broken. As we sat in the driveway in silence, a flood of emotions rushed over us. We were feeling a mixture of relief, anger, bitterness, regret, and a passionate desire for revenge. My eyes burned with tears as I allowed myself to remember and feel the pain of the past. The things we had tried so hard to forget were now a raw and present reality.

I fought the lump in my throat not wanting Amanda to see me cry. I sat and wept silently. It was late fall and the chill outside matched the cold atmosphere of my truck. Out of the corner of my eye, I noticed her reaching into her coat pocket and pulling out a tissue. She wiped her cheeks then her hand fell aimlessly into her lap.

What are we supposed to do now?

There we sat together, grieving silently but separately. I slowly reached across the console and took her hand, and for the very first time, we prayed together. I don't remember all the words of the prayer, but it doesn't matter.

It was short and it was real.

Both of us felt so defeated—beyond hope, useless and helpless. But with all the brokenness and difficult emotions we were feeling, we simply said, "Lord, if there is anything You can use our lives for in Your kingdom, here we are."

We both said "Amen" then went inside.

I wasn't sure how to bridle the flood of emotions; probably a guy's worst nightmare is to keep looking strong when he feels totally weak.

During the first couple of months in my newfound faith, I acted shamefully in saying some very unkind things to people around me—things that came out of my own concealed pain.

Ultimately, my pastor rebuked me gently. He admonished me to live out my faith and trust God for the healing that would come in due time.

I also came to realize that scripture says, "Dearly beloved, avenge not yourselves, but rather give place unto wrath: for it is written, Vengeance is mine; I will repay, saith the Lord" (Romans 12:19 KJV).

I came to realize that I needed to release the offenders to Jesus. I could never bring my perpetrators to repentance and, as long as I tried to, I would be the one to carry bitterness and hatred. The best thing for me to do was to be honest with Jesus—about the agony they had caused me—and then leave them at the foot of the cross.

Jesus is perfectly capable of convicting them as He sees fit.

I also needed to accept the fact that those people might never repent. But even if they didn't, I would keep praying for them and keep releasing them to Jesus when my negative emotions arose.

Though I was dealing with the offenses of others in my life, there was something even bigger that continued to nag—the many people I had hurt over the years. I felt a desperate need for the healing and forgiveness of God for those transgressions, as well.

In no way do I mean to make this process sound easy. I've struggled tremendously over the years to maintain this right position in Jesus. Yes, I have sometimes failed, but by God's grace...

... I always return to His will.

PLAIN LESSON FOR LIFE

Emotional Wounds Can Heal

Our emotional and internal wounds are much like a cut or gash on our physical body. Imagine that you had an encounter that left you with a minor cut on your arm. Chances are, you can leave it and it will heal itself and disappear over the next few days. Let's suppose that instead of a minor cut, you received a significant wound. This one left to itself will likely turn red, get sore, and become infected. But a few minor treatments of cleaning it out, putting some salve on it, and topping it with a bandage, and you're good to go.

Now, let's imagine receiving a gash half the length of your forearm and clear to the bone. I think we would agree that this one exceeds your medical abilities and you need a doctor—not tomorrow, but today!

You'll have to go through the painful process of removing all the excess blood, dirt, and ruined skin, cleaning the wound to prepare it for healing, having it closed artificially, then heavily bandaged. In the physical world, we treat the three wounds differently because of their severity.

We understand this perfectly in the natural and physical world. Whether it's applied to man or beast, it makes sense. But in our human reasoning, we sometimes have a "disconnect" when it comes to matters of the heart and soul.

When someone experiences sexual assault or physical, verbal, or mental abuse, we tend to think that they should forget it, not talk about it, and move on. We sometimes even ask, what's the benefit of bringing up the past? There can be an assumption that when bringing up past traumatic events, we're looking for someone to blame.

I admit that when Amanda and I finished our counseling sessions, that's exactly what I had in mind. In my emotional turmoil, I made statements and acted out in ways that I was very ashamed of and needed to apologize for. A dear friend helped me see that the purpose for going back and bringing up the past wasn't to allocate blame, but rather to...

- Identify the wound and the pain
- Understand how the wound affects our lives
- Ask the Healer to heal the internal wound
- Forgive and pray for the offender

Once we gain fresh perspective of the wound—how it works and how it causes us to react—we can start recognizing our responses to situations and begin changing them to align with God's will for our lives. This is when our journey to healing really begins.

He heals the brokenhearted
and binds up their wounds. (Psalms 147:3 ESV)

Chapter Twenty-Two

NEW LIFE, OLD HABITS

No doubt, our lives had changed dramatically. God was convicting Amanda and me of sin, and we were committed to aligning our hearts with His Word. When we failed (and we certainly did), our new daring challenge was to not walk away from our faith like before, but to go back to our Heavenly Father through prayer.

Even now, I believe our Heavenly Father looks on with pleasure at newborn believers who are delighted to follow Him. Most people want to see God do great things, but often He does those great things on the platform of a trial or test.

Amanda and I both had some financial trouble we were trying to rise above, and my situation was getting worrisome. One morning, when I came home from trucking for a few days, I found an invoice that Amanda had left for me that needed to be paid right away.

Guess what... I didn't have the money.

Since there was no one else at home with me, I did something I had never done before: I fell on my face on the living room floor and called out to my Heavenly Father. I confessed to Him that I had made bad decisions and had gotten myself into serious trouble. I also confessed that I desperately needed His help.

As much as I wanted to just rest and trust that God was bigger than this problem, I struggled.

What was I going to do?

Since I was leaving on another job that night, I needed to be getting some sleep. But the anxiety kept me awake. *Maybe I should call someone and borrow enough money to pay the bill.*

The hours passed as I paced nervously back and forth in that mobile home. Suddenly, my thoughts were interrupted by a car slowing on the road outside. When I pulled the blinds open and peered outside, I was just in time to see the mail truck drive away.

As I scanned the envelopes, I noticed one with a return address from someone in Daviess County—my home community. I quickly tore it open to find a check made out to me. It was from a friend that owed me money that I had totally forgotten about.

Would you believe that the amount was enough to pay the bill that was due with still some left over to put into my bank account!

God answers prayer retroactively!

In his omnipresence, he hears the prayer before we pray it, and answers it before we need it.

What an incredible faith-builder!

†††

While my faith was growing, the battle for my soul was ongoing. Out of all the things I needed redemption from, my addiction to tobacco was probably the greatest battle I fought. Yes, I said that I threw away two packs of cigarettes when I became born again, but they call it a "stronghold" for a reason. It's usually something so embedded in your psyche, it refuses to give up the ground.

Since I started using it when I was quite young, it had created a stronghold deep in my being. It was the very first thing I reached for in the morning and the last thing I used before going to bed at night.

Truck driving possibly made my struggle even worse. I normally smoked to stay awake when traveling long hours, but now I was always munching on whatever I could find.

Often, when people are trying to stop a habit, they turn to something to take their minds off the thing they are trying to stop.

I turned toward food.

I had a small refrigerator in the sleeper of my semi-truck. When the temptation for a cigarette got intense, I reached for my ultimate comfort food—a rich, creamy chocolate milk and caramel candy bar. You know the one with those little squares filled with all that golden, gooey happiness!

Suddenly, I realized my clothes were all too small, so I criticized my roommate's laundry techniques.

"The water you're using must be insanely hot or your dryer settings are wrong," I said.

"Why?" he asked with a sheepish grin.

"My clothes have all shrunk!" I replied, nowhere near close enough to admitting the actual truth.

He threw his head back and howled with laughter! "My clothes still fit just fine!" he crowed.

My sudden packing on of thirty whopping pounds was evident to everyone except me. It appeared I had traded one obsession for another.

I was starting to believe I would never be free from that nasty tobacco, no matter how many pounds I put on. I would make it a few days without a cigarette before nearly jumping out of my skin. Then I'd give in and buy a pack believing that satisfaction would surely to come.

Of course, it didn't.

Mere minutes after lighting that first one, I would feel so guilty that I ended up throwing the rest of the pack into the garbage. A few days later, I would repeat the whole thing over again.

That agonizing cycle went on for several months.

In the midst of my fight for dominion over smoking, Amanda seemed to consistently be in a bad mood. She cried a lot; maybe just discouraged, I thought.

One day, we had some errands to run. I let her know I would pick her up after work and we'd spend some time together. I felt sure that after a nice evening of encouragement, she'd be happy again. Maybe it's a guy thing... we just have to fix things.

We hadn't even made it to the restaurant when my attempts at lightening her spirit was met with tears. She was crying again. I couldn't believe it!

Okay, I needed to stay patient, but I intended to find out what was going on. I reached over and took her hand.

"Sweets, what wrong?"

"Nothing," she replied as she stared straight ahead. With an occasional sniffle as she wiped her eyes and silence prevailing, I began to lose my cool.

"What's wrong?" I asked, this time with some force. She fidgeted with the damp tissue.

"I don't know," she whispered.

"What?" I exclaimed! "You mean to tell me that you've been sullen for the past few days and cried nonstop for the past twenty minutes, and you don't know why you are doing it"? I was done.

Frustrated, I pulled my hand from hers and promptly placed it on the steering wheel with my other one. Now it was my turn. I steamed quietly.

"Please, don't be angry with me," she pleaded. "I'll be okay. I just need some time."

My frustration grew. "I just don't understand how a person can cry and not know the reason for it," I muttered.

Then it suddenly hit me. She was going to break up with me! Really? Was that possible? Would she really do that?

My anger melted into fear as I pondered the idea. What would I do? My mind ran wild with all the possibilities until I couldn't take it anymore.

Removing my right hand from its tight grip on the wheel, I reached over and slipped it into hers again. She squeezed it.

"Amanda," I said timidly, "are you going to break up with me?"

"Oh, no!" she exclaimed as she squeezed my hand even tighter. "I love you. I just need some time to think and clear my head. I'll be okay very soon, I promise."

Thank God. I would try to be patient and give her the time she needed.

A few days later as I was arriving home from work, my phone rang and it was Amanda. She sounded a bit better, but still seemed tired.

"Can you come over tonight? I need to talk with you about something."

"Sure, Sweets," I said. "I'll be over in a bit."

It took only a few minutes to dress and drive to her apartment. I had mixed feelings. On one hand I was relieved because it seemed like I was finally going to get to the bottom of what was bothering her. On the other hand, I was anxious about hearing what in the world it could be.

When I walked in, she was sitting on the bed with a pile of damp tissues beside her. Her face was pale and her eyes red from crying.

Then, she smiled.

Whoa, I didn't see that coming!

Now, I was really interested in hearing what she had to say.

"What's on your mind, Sweets?" I asked hesitantly as I took off my jacket and hung it.

She repositioned herself and motioned for me to come sit next to her. She took my hand, paused for a minute then removed a strand of blonde hair from her face.

"I'm happy and I'm sad."

Oh, great. We were right back where we were a few nights ago. With the bloodshot eyes and this abstract statement, I was sure her waterworks would start again anytime.

"I'm sad because of doing something I regret, and I'm happy because I'm experiencing something I thought God would never allow me to experience." She said it as she fought back the tears. "People have told me I never would get this honor, and I was sure God felt the same way."

She had my full attention. I scooted to the edge of the bed as I sharply turned and looked at her. "What ever could you be talking about?"

She hesitated for a moment, turned and looked at me.

"Amos, I'm pregnant."

CHANNEL OF PRAYER

Everywhere I go I can find advice

And to have a friends shoulder, sometimes it sure is nice

When they don't understand, or even seem to care

I can talk to Jesus, through the channel of prayer

Chorus

When I meet Jesus and I see His smiling face

When I meet Jesus oh there's no sweeter place

I tell Him my feelings; He loves it when we share
When I meet Jesus through the channel of prayer

He's my best friend and He never lets me down
He said if I would come He would in no wise cast me out
When the phones all are busy and nobody's there
I have direct connection through the channel of prayer
You can talk to Jesus through the channel of prayer

—Amos Raber Jr.

Chapter Twenty-Three

FINDING HOME

Yes, previously Amanda and I had both lived immoral life styles, but after our new birth in Christianity, we had purposed purity in our courtship—a new leaf. And we were successful until we went to visit someone in another community. The opportunity arose like a storm and we were too weak to withstand the temptation.

And we gave in.

Now, we were pregnant!

Even before this, we deeply regretted our decision and were devastated by our actions. Now, we had failed in the worst way. We were both sorry for what we had done, but this was something we weren't ready for.

What about our church family? They had gone above and beyond in showing kindness to us, and this was certainly no way to repay them. What were we going to do now? What about our professed new faith that we were so excited about? Would they still accept us like before?

But no matter what the outcome, we had to tell them. We were deeply ashamed, and the thought of letting everyone down was crushing. But there was no other choice. We simply had to be honest.

We would tell them everything.

† † †

The appointed evening came when it was time to spill the beans. We knew our pastor and ministers were going to be disappointed, and perhaps even angry—they had every right to be. I dreaded the thought of what their reaction would be to our news. They couldn't help but feel incredibly let down.

Why wouldn't they be?

To our surprise, they graciously heard us out to the end while their countenance revealed compassion.

"We all make mistakes that we're not proud of," said one of them. He continued, "Yes, you have fallen, but at this point, that isn't the most important thing. The most important question is, what will you do about it?"

I couldn't believe they took the "neither do I condemn you; go and sin no more" approach. Then they explained the repentance and forgiveness concept, telling us stories about people in the Bible who had fallen into a variety of sins, but when they came to Jesus, they found Him ready and willing to forgive and restore them.

That was hard to believe or imagine. How would we ever be able to rid ourselves of the guilt that would surely follow us always?

Since we were new to praying from our heart as well as out loud, they offered to lead us through a prayer of repentance to ask for God's forgiveness through Jesus.

After saying this amazing prayer, though the regret was still very real, the guilt was gone! We were ready to except God's forgiveness and move on.

Scripture says that "the righteous may fall seven times but arises again" (Proverbs 24:16), and "he that covereth his sins shall not prosper, but whoso confesseth and forsaketh them shall have mercy" (Proverbs 28:13).

The moment was bittersweet.

†††

For mid-November in Northern Indiana, it was a sunny day. I was coming out of Chicago with a load of steel coils on my semi. Traffic flowed well that morning, and it looked like I would be home at a decent hour, maybe even in time for dinner with my sweetheart.

Waiting till I knew she would be on her lunch break, I called her.

"Hey, Sweets, would you mind if a guy like me would come to your apartment and join you for dinner tonight?"

"Sure," she said. "You just come right on over."

"What's for dinner?" I asked.

"Well, Mr. Raber," she said with a smirk, "maybe I just want to surprise you."

Surprise huh? She doesn't have a clue. I thought smugly.

I arrived home right on schedule, parked the semi, and got ready for a Friday night dinner with my Sweets.

After the twenty minute drive to her apartment, I slowly opened the door and peeped around the corner where Amanda stood in the kitchen with her back turned toward me.

Perfect!

I tiptoed quietly across the floor and stopped several feet behind her.

"Amanda Byler," I said softly.

She spun around quickly and her hands flew to her mouth when she saw me on one knee.

"Will you marry me?"

If her expression held her answer, I knew I was about to become the most fortunate man alive.

"Yes, Mr. Raber!" she exclaimed. "I will marry you!"

Right there in her little apartment kitchen with the smell of spaghetti hanging in the air, we hugged as an engaged couple. We were getting married!

The wedding date was set: December 21.

† † †

In the coming days, Amanda made what seemed like an endless amount of phone calls to tell all her friends about the wedding!

The planning was under way.

She had such an amazing time going over all the details. Me—I was simply glad I would be the groom.

This was a turning point for me. I needed a change, a career change.

Through one of our pastors, I found out about a job at a feed mill in Wakarusa.

Since I had just moved to the area, I didn't realize how far the drive would be, but if it meant I could be home every night, it was worth a daily forty-minute drive. When I met Mr. Frank Martin, he took me through a short interview and I left, optimistic.

Soon the phone call came, and Frank said I could have the job if I wanted it. So, just a few weeks before the wedding, I started as an employee at Wakarusa Nutritional.

As a part of my pay, Frank offered us a house to live in after we were married. I refer to it as my "Walky Home."

We had just crossed two big obstacles in one jump: I had found a day job, and now we had an actual house instead of the apartment.

Amanda loved that cute little house. It was small, but it was home—home for her, me, and our baby.

† † †

There were a few things that both of us wanted for the special day, but mostly we just wanted to share it with our friends.

Amanda dreamed of an ivory and cream dress with elegant buttons down the back. I remember the day we went to a local flower shop to order the flowers. She was after white roses with blue baby's breath, and she insisted that I wear them on my vest. That thought always frightened me—getting poked when they attempted to fasten it.

My only request for the wedding was that I wanted my favorite dish, Haystack, for lunch and to have my singing friends from my home community to come and share some songs on our special day.

Let me explain for those of you unfamiliar with the dish Haystack, which was one of my favorite meals from my childhood. It's a dish that lived up to its name—a challenge of sorts.

With an empty plate, preferably a big one, we would start by creating a bed of lettuce, then crumbled chips on top, then rice, and finally ground beef. This is typically when the challenge began, when you still needed to make room for salsa, sour cream, and melted cheese.

Amanda insisted that the Haystack menu options include chopped hard-boiled eggs, which threw the food committee for a loop. But, as expected, the bride and groom won.

The big day finally arrived.

Friends and family came from different communities to witness the beginning of our new life together. There was lots of laughter and reminiscing with old friends, and of course, lots of photos taken. The lunch was as delicious as the idea had promised.

I couldn't believe it... we were married!

When it was all over, Amanda and I left that little church behind and sped off to begin our honeymoon.

Home!

I know what you're thinking, but it was Amanda who chose the location.

"I want to go home and spend time with my family."

After she said it and I had a chance to think it over, I wasn't so surprised. As I mentioned earlier, she had been away from her family for quite some time. Now, after reuniting with them over the past year, she couldn't get enough of them.

Her childhood seemed closer than ever—the excitement and joy was overwhelming and deeply felt.

So, off we went to Clare, Michigan.

When we arrived in Clare, Amanda was excited to show me her room from when she was a little girl. She giggled gleefully as she shared memories from the past. We even slept in her old bedroom and got up late, spending the mornings with her parents eating the family's traditional breakfasts and talking about the years gone by.

Throughout the day, we visited friends and went to see more family at lunch time. While driving through the community, we saw the little Amish school Amanda attended while growing up. We stopped for a few minutes and watched as the children played.

But it was the evenings that were the most memorable. After dinner, Amanda and her mother stood side-by-side washing the dishes and laughing as they recalled bygone days. Her dad and I sat in the living room sipping coffee and smiling as we watched the ladies. It was quite entertaining.

After a while, the gals joined us and we visited until the wee hours of the morning. Oh, the joy and bliss of watching my wife's face as she laughed at the silly stories that were shared. We ended by discussing some scripture verses and then knelt as her dad prayed.

It was a perfect picture of reconciliation.

After spending a few days with her family, we traveled to the nearest city, found a nice hotel, and spent some time alone before heading back to Indiana. Money was tight, so we stopped at several hotels before finding one that we could afford.

I remember the pride I felt when going inside each one, getting the price, then telling the clerk that I needed to check with my wife. It had a nice ring to it.

For a few weeks prior to the wedding and up to this time, Amanda was emotional, something I now realize was partially due to her pregnancy. But due to my lack of head knowledge on the subject, I didn't understand that.

As I mentioned earlier, though my conversion was real and God had shown Himself to be strong on my behalf, I was slowly starting to backslide into the person I had been before—selfishness and pride were beginning to take over again.

We finally decided on a hotel and got settled in. Not long afterwards, we had a small disagreement that grew out of proportion. After a lengthy and intense argument, I angrily got up and left the room muttering under my breath. I walked to the parking lot, got into my truck, and sped off.

As I drove aimlessly around town, I was easily overcome by the old desires that used to dictate my behavior. I was tempted to find a bar and drink the night away, but I settled on a calmer option.

Whipping into a convenient store, I bought a pack of cigarettes and drove around trying to settle the unrest in my soul. Long after midnight, I went back to the hotel and my new wife.

I expected to find Amanda asleep or possibly angry with me, but as I quietly slipped in the door, she warmly greeted me with tear-filled eyes. We knelt and prayed together, leaving me ashamed of my inability to maturely deal with even the slightest conflict without racing out the door.

To wallow in my anger, self-pity, and cigarettes was not the kind of husband I wanted to be.

I promised Amanda that I would never again storm out on her.

I realized I had to find home.

Chapter Twenty-Four

TOO SOON FOR GOODBYE

The next few days of our honeymoon were much better, but my actions the night I walked out had created a fear in me.

I was amazed and ashamed at how quickly I'd given in to my own struggles, willing to leave my bride crying and alone. What was I capable of? Was this new faith really changing me or was it a mind game that I was playing? Would I ever really be different? I contemplated our future and my ability to care for my wife and our coming child.

†††

When the time came for us to go back to Indiana, Amanda and I drove out to the Clare Amish community to say goodbye to her family. After hearty hugs, we were off.

In many ways, life was now just starting for us. We chatted freely as we drove the three-hour trip back to Indiana, reminiscing about the time spent with her loved ones.

"Just think," she said with a twinkle in her eye, "soon we'll be making the trip again, but with a baby!"

It was such a thrilling thought. The two of us were about to become three.

We stopped along Highway 127 for a break and to get some lunch at a sandwich shop. We talked about lots of things that day, but none more important than her not going back to work in the woodworking shop where she'd been for the previous six months. I hardly gave it another thought since I wasn't sure if she was talking about changing jobs or possibly preparing to be a stay-at-home mother.

Getting back home meant that it was time to move her things from her apartment into my house—the Walky Home.

†††

"I'm okay," I protested. "I just want to be with my wife!"

"Mr., Raber," the paramedic said, "we know you think you're okay, but we need to check you out to make sure."

Reluctantly, I watched as they slid Amanda into the back of the emergency vehicle, shutting the door behind them. Then they sped away, sirens screaming as they disappeared into the fog.

They carefully hurried me to the other ambulance, and swiftly took off for Elkhart General Hospital.

I was fully awake listening to the eerie sound of the sirens as we made our way through the countryside then onto State Road 19. I asked repeatedly about Amanda's condition, but they could offer no information.

When we reached the hospital, they rushed me in through the emergency entrance and into a room. A panel of tests came fast and furious.

Soon, the doctors confirmed that, despite my soreness, I only had a few minor injuries. My body needed to recover from the trauma, but I would be fine.

Now I would just need to wait for Amanda in the waiting room and we would be on our way home.

Home... I just wanted to get home. To empty her apartment, to move her into our new house. To really start our life together. But the nervous looks I saw in the eyes of the nurses made me doubt myself.

"The doctor will be here to talk with you soon," was all they said as they hurried off. I tried to reassure myself that Amanda would be okay. Bad things always happen to other people, but not us.

Not us.

My thoughts were interrupted by some of our pastoral team that had arrived. By evening, several other friends from church and some of Amanda's family were at the hospital.

And after all the initial tests and scans had been done, the doctor was ready to sit down and explain the situation.

"Imagine taking a single peanut, putting it into a jar, and shaking it as violently as possible. That is what happened to your wife's brain. It isn't damaged in just one place; it's swollen due to trauma all around it."

"But she's three months pregnant."

I thought there had to be some mistake. This wasn't cancer or some other terminal disease, just an accident.

Numbness enveloped me as the doctor went on to explain that her chances for survival were slim, and even if she did live, her brain injury would likely render her helpless in many ways. Currently, she was being sustained by life support.

It was like the sky fell on me and there was no one big enough or strong enough to put it back.

God... where are you right now?

†††

After a few hours of getting the news, Pastor Loren and his wife, Esther, encouraged me to leave the hospital and go get a shower and change of clothes.

The long night hours finally turned into morning with no real change in Amanda's condition. I sat in the waiting room with some of her family, but conversation was futile. We all had one question and one question only: Would she be okay?

At the ping of the elevator bell, we lifted our weary heads to see who had come.

"Mom... Dad!" I exclaimed as I got up to greet them.

We embraced and wept.

My parents, sister, my brothers and their wives had all come to be with us. What a comfort to have them there with me.

Another meeting with the doctors told us that nothing had changed; they didn't seem to have much hope. But they offered to keep her on life support for some time if that was what we wanted.

That wasn't just another patient in that room, it was my bride and my unborn child.

I wanted her back. I wanted them back.

Chapter Twenty-Five

SHORT MISSION

There we sat numb with the surreal reality that Amanda was on life support, and there wasn't a thing I could do about it.

"Amos, you're her husband; the final decision is up to you. We'll support you either way."

Amanda's father was never one to mince words, and what he said frightened me. The woman who had given birth to Amanda was there, and the man who had been her daddy all her life was there, and they were acknowledging that the decision regarding their daughter's life rested on my shoulders. I had only been her husband for nine days. How could I possibly meet that responsibility?

I couldn't believe this was happening. How could my whole life—my whole world—boil down to such a sudden and implausible scenario? How could the life of my wife, our baby, and our entire future be hanging in the balance, in my hands?

After hours of silent praying, pleading, and contemplating, I made the choice.

I would take Amanda off life support, giving her back to the One who created her—her one true parent.

But first, I asked to be left alone with her, uninterrupted by anyone.

† † †

She was as graceful and lovely as ever lying there peacefully, only the sound of the respirator clicking and heaving quietly. She didn't make a sound, didn't move. I sat down next to her and took her hand.

"Hey, Sweets, it's me," I said as if speaking on a long distance call. There but faraway.

"I just wanted to come and visit with you a bit."

Then, I started at the beginning of our relationship, recalling lots of special times—from the day we'd met almost one year before to the present.

And as I spoke to her, my mind wandered...

I saw us together, laughing and talking as we gleefully held hands walking together as we so often did. Eventually we came to a river. It was peaceful and gentle as its waters flowed downstream. We stood stationary for a minute watching the current for a while, but somehow we both knew that she needed to go. She and our baby.

We lingered reluctantly as I gripped her hand tightly.

"Sweets, I love you so much, and I really am sorry for hurting you on our honeymoon. Thank you for being so kind and patient with me. I don't want you to go. I want to see the baby, cradle it in my arms, and then watch it grow. But if you must leave, I want to release you. I'll be okay. Go on and rest, and I'll join you later."

She looked at me with a war of emotions in her eyes, and I could see she was anxious, but it was overshadowed by a glimmer of excitement.

"I'm afraid," she whispered as she gripped my hand. "What if I can't make it across? Can you help me?"

"No, I can't help you this time, Sweets," I replied. "But there is no need to worry. Jesus will be right there to carry you and our little baby safely across."

† † †

A sudden noise in the hospital hallway jolted me back to where she was, lying there in her bed. Just silently lying there with me sitting by her side still holding her hand.

"Hey, Sweets, if you can hear me and if you're able, can you give my hand a squeeze?"

I waited for what seemed like several minutes, then suddenly and ever so slightly, her little finger twitched in my hand.

"Thank you," I whispered with tears threatening.

I lingered as I fondly gazed upon the girl I loved so much. Finally, I leaned over her, gave her one last kiss, and then turned to leave the room. I stopped and looked back one final time at what appeared to be her sleeping so soundly. I hoped by some miracle she would call my name and tell me it was all okay, but she didn't.

Numb with pain and sorrow, I slowly closed the door behind me and walked the long hallway toward the waiting room where I knew our families and friends were expecting me. My footsteps echoed as I recalled the day before as Amanda and I dreamed of our whole life ahead of us. Today, it was all becoming one more memory to cling to.

Minutes later, the life support was turned off and Amanda slipped away into eternity.

My wife—my Sweets—and baby were gone.

Our child with the tiny face I would never see, the soft bundle I would never hold, the life I would never know.

It was New Year's Day

We were married for eleven days.

†††

My heart seemed to explode with desperation. If I couldn't live life with her, I wanted to join her.

The pastoral team told me we needed to go to the funeral home and make the arrangements. I was dazed. It was like waking up from a bad dream, only it didn't stop. It just kept going.

We rode in silence to Nappanee where we were met by a kind man, but there to do business. With pen and paper in hand, he asked multiple questions, and the tension rose in my heart.

I can't do this! my heart screamed. I wasn't ready to believe she was gone, let alone start making decisions about what kind of casket to bury her in!

The visitation hours were set and soon family and friends were gathering again at Fairview Mennonite Church—the same country church where we had exchanged our vows just days before.

The church building and the fellowship hall were right across the road from each other on a small county road, south of Nappanee Indiana. On our wedding day, we held the ceremony in the church building and then had walked across the road to enjoy the Haystack lunch in the fellowship hall.

This day, we prepared both buildings to say goodbye to Amanda.

My mind flooded with images too recent to believe that they were now only memories. This was the place we had driven by Sunday after Sunday trying to decide if this was the church for us. The church building where Amanda prayed to receive Jesus in her heart and was then baptized. The place where these people loved us and patiently cared for us as young Christians.

There were just too many good times here. It was like a beautiful work of art, and now somehow it seemed impossible, even wrong to have it tainted with such sadness.

In the distance, we saw the hearse coming. It pulled into the driveway and the funeral directors carried the casket in to prepare for the visitation hours. We waited for the coffin to be opened so we could have a few last moments of viewing her body.

There she was, as splendid as ever, wearing the ivory and cream wedding dress—her dream dress.

The visitation days and hours were tiring, but also encouraging as droves of people came from everywhere to show their support and to honor my young wife.

The funeral day held so many mourners that two services ran simultaneously. Pastor Loren and Amanda's Amish uncle, Toby Detweiler, spoke in the church building while Randy Miller and Lotus Kuhns, both home ministers at Fairview, spoke in the fellowship hall.

Our friends that served in the wedding party were there to help in any way they could. The wedding singers were also there, but this time they sang songs about Heaven. Amanda's new home.

Soon, the services were over and it was time to move to the cemetery for the final ceremony and burial. It was a cold day in Northern Indiana. Family, relatives, and friends from near and far huddled together attempting to block off the frigid northwest wind and the flurries that fell aimlessly around us. But we hardly noticed. The dark, gaping hole in front of us made sure of that.

So cold, so merciless, so final.

The frozen ground was a true resemblance of the chill we were experiencing in our hearts. Silence was the dominate presence with the occasional baby crying or someone sniffling.

This was it. This was the finale of her life on earth. Amanda was young and vital with a smile that wasn't easily forgotten. In many ways, her life had just begun with more reasons to live than she ever had before.

The crowd slowly dispersed leaving only the family at the church. It was evening—the evening of January 4th—precisely one year after our first date.

† † †

Amanda's brother, Ivan, had friends with a toddler that were there at the gravesite. A few weeks later in their home in Michigan, the little boy was with his mother as she cleaned the attic when she came across a box of Christmas decorations. In it were several angel ornaments. As they were admiring them, the mother asked the little guy if he knew what they were.

"Yes," he replied. "Those are just like the ones I saw in the sky while we put Ivan's sister in the ground."

Like an exquisite rainbow shines after a storm, the little boy's revelation felt like a message directly from God.

Yes, the storm was severe and my life looked bleak, but none of it was actually out of control. The One who created it all, including the storm, was faithfully residing over every detail.

Amanda's vision and hope was that she would be instrumental in helping at least one person find the peace she'd found in Jesus. On the day of her funeral, salvation was clearly preached.

To our knowledge, forty people young and old prayed to receive Jesus as their Savior.

Amanda was perhaps as effective in nine days as any missionary has ever been.

Chapter Twenty-Six

REST IN THE EYE OF THE STORM

I crashed. I wept for hours, sometimes finding myself in a fetal position. Close friends, including the late David Miller, aka Singer David Miller, stayed with me for several nights. They hurt, cried, and prayed alongside me. They listened and cared while I crumbled.

I lost my will to live.

My condition was alarming, so much so that some people thought I might be suicidal. I wasn't, I simply wanted to be in Heaven with my wife, my baby, and Redeemer. Earthly things had no appeal. I woke every day thinking that today might be the day that Jesus would call me home. Perhaps the trumpet would sound or I'd fall over dead. Maybe I'd have an accident. All felt like welcomed options.

I just wanted to go Home.

The day came for me to move into the house where Amanda and I had planned to live—where we were headed on the day of the accident—the

Wakarusa house. Yes, I knew my church family loved me dearly, and they showed it by providing meals and support. But they couldn't be by my side 24/7. The time had come for me to face the nights alone.

The next few months proved to be some of the most challenging times of my life. When I returned to work, it took my mind off my sorrow. I asked my employer for more hours since the time between 5pm and 8am was the part of the day I dreaded the most.

Throughout the day, my mind raced from one duty to the next as I fulfilled my delivery responsibilities and was around other people. But when the day ended and I made the three-mile drive home, I knew that only silence and long hours awaited me.

I grew up in a family of six children and wasn't used to being alone in a quiet house. The days dragged on, but they weren't as bad as the nights that seemed to last forever.

I paced the floor, cried, and prayed. But nothing I did seemed to help. At last, the sleepless nights caught up with me as I struggled to stay awake at work. I was totally exhausted.

Working at the feed mill and dealing with my grief created a physical strain on my body. I loved the hard work of maneuvering fifty-pound bags of feed all day long, but without sleep and barely eating, it proved to be too much. I began to lose weight and became weaker and weaker.

It was a hot day in early June, six months after the accident, when the supporting people around me naturally started moving on to other things. I felt the pressure to become normal again—to move on with them.

For the most part, I was well on my way, but this was a particularly hard day—one of those days when everything seemed very raw.

I had the truck loaded, ready for the next delivery. All I needed was a few bags from the warehouse. I began carrying them one by one to the truck, but I crumbled in despair right on the pallet of feedbags and did what I hadn't done for a few weeks.

I wept.

I'm not sure how long I stayed there or whether some unsuspecting customer fled from the scene when they discovered a male employee crying.

My sleep deprivation continued to drive me closer to insanity. I even bought a sleeping aid, but it didn't seem to help. A friend suggested I talk to a naturopath at Northern Nutrition in Shipshewana, and I agreed since I was desperate to try anything.

After hearing my story over the phone, Dr. Kevin told me to buy a bottle of Vitamin B Complex and take them aggressively until I was able to sleep. He explained that due to all the trauma I'd experienced, he believed that my adreno/nerve system was depleted and needed to be revitalized. And he was right! After a few days, I was able to sleep all night. What a blessing! My physical batteries were recharged!

†††

In the midst of all the turmoil, my faith was renewed though my heart was still shattered. Some of the strongest roots of my faith today still come from the darkest moments of those days—coming home from work drained and mentally shot. Countless times I came through the door and fell flat on my face as I cried out to God in my desperation.

I was honest with the Almighty, my Heavenly Father. He could have struck me dead for showing such anger and frustration. I asked Him again and again why He had to take Amanda from me. Instead, I experienced a kind, loving, and patient Father who quietly carried me through those deep valleys. I rose and fell like a yoyo, but no matter how rocky my days were, He was always my Safe Place, my Refuge.

My greatest fear during that time was that I would revert to my old lifestyle of alcohol, tobacco and immorality; that I would slip into a dark hole of hopelessness.

My greatest hope and desire was that God would use my experiences to help others and further His kingdom.

I found that playing my guitar and singing became incredibly meaningful therapy for me. Within the first few weeks after the funeral, I'd already written several songs.

†††

Two weeks after the funeral, I got a phone call from a pastor friend in my home community. He invited me to come to their church and share my story. Looking back now, I can hardly believe I did it. But it proved to be enormously healing.

People respond differently in times of loss—some want to talk about it and others bury it all inside. I found that talking about it was like a salve. I welcomed the many phone calls that came over the next several months, which allowed multiple opportunities to share my story with people everywhere.

One day while driving, I remembered the song that Amanda and I had written together as she rode with me on a weekend truck run. It was a typical love gone bad country song, but as I thought about the words and realized with some minor tweaking, it would fit my situation perfectly.

MIDNIGHT HOUR

Lying alone midnight hour
Praying for my sleep to come
My empty arms are tired and aching
Trying to believe that you're gone

1st Chorus

You went and left me here a crying all alone
I just can't understand why you had to go
I know your patiently waiting for me
And Honey we'll spend all eternity

My mind goes back to a song we loved to sing
Your favorite song, The Comforter has come
My Lord and Savior in the Spirit
He's always near and He's never wrong

2nd Chorus
He comforts me while I'm crying all alone
He helps me understand why you had to go
He says you're patiently waiting just for me
And together we'll spend all eternity

And we'll never part again He's promised me
And Honey we'll spend all eternity

—Amos Raber Jr.

Though there was still a dark cloud hanging over me, it wasn't as bad as before. But the truth was, I was still struggling with quitting smoking. Alcohol and other strongholds had fallen like broken chains since that awesome day in August, but not this nasty smoking habit. It held on like a barnacle to a ship's hull.

Over the fifteen years of being a slave to this fixation, I had tried numerous times to quit only to hear friends say, "Once a smoker, always a smoker. You'll never quit!"

There were a few positive voices, but they were certainly drowned out by the hopeless ones.

Every few days, the pressure would win and I would walk into the store—in complete denial—and buy one more pack of smokes and a lighter. Outside, I would franticly open it, unable to wait to light up and feel the nicotine hit my lungs.

Repeatedly, the need to satisfy the urge was met with the same end: defeat, disappointment, and misery. I was left sitting there with the full realization that I had fallen, yet again, facing the same results as the time before.

Ashamed and slightly dizzy from the nicotine, I wasn't used to it anymore. I'd walk over to the dumpster and drop my $6.50 failure in the trash.

"Oh, God," I cried, "will I ever be free from this captivity?"

I believed that God created the heavens and the earth, and had the ability to save my soul. Could He not set me free from this one stubborn stronghold?

It was in February when I was invited to a church to share my testimony. As I drove home alone late that night, I felt the strong urge to stop and buy cigarettes, so I did.

Obviously, I wanted to enjoy them, but I didn't.

Just like so many times before, I felt empty, defeated, and like I had disappointed my Heavenly Father. As I sat there in the front seat of my truck thinking about what had just happened, I experienced my very first discipline from the Lord.

"The Lord disciplines those he loves, as a father the son he delights in" (Proverbs 3:12 NIV).

Then the Lord spoke to me through the Holy Spirit in a gentle but firm tone.

"Amos, you need to choose between me and the cigarettes. If you continue to fill your body with smoke, I will no longer pour my Spirit on you."

Like the Bible says, "Do you not know that your body is a temple of the Holy Spirit within you, whom you have from God? You are not your own, for you were bought with a price. So glorify God in your body" (I Cor. 6:19-20 ESV)

I had never experienced anything like this before.

I drove the rest of the way home in deep contemplation.

By the time I pulled into the driveway, I was convinced that I needed serious help with this intense struggle. I also knew that due to countless times of trying to quit and failing, I would never be able to master this mountain on my own.

I went inside feeling the heaviness of the situation, I again fell on my face crying out to God for help! When I finished praying, He invited me to go further by faith—by the power of the Holy Spirit—to commit to never smoking again.

The thought alone frightened me; the past few months didn't offer a lot of hope! What if I failed again? Why wouldn't I fail again?

Then I sensed a rest and bidding to trust God. There I stood, and with a mix of fear and excitement said, "Dear Lord, I promise from this day forward, I will never smoke again."

I prayed it from the heart—from my own personal faith level—to a merciful Father that asks us to abide in His love. Not in the world; not in things of the world, but solely and completely in Him.

I wondered what I had just done.

I arose the next day a bit skeptical, but tried to have faith that all would be well. Days turned into weeks, and weeks into months as God proved to have set me free by faith and confession!

I'm here to testify that to this day, more than fourteen years later, not one cigarette has touched these lips! The battle was real, but so was the amazing grace and strength of God!

All I had to do was rest. Rest in the support of those caring individuals around me. Rest knowing that sometimes the troubles of life are beyond our own strength. Rest in the sanctuary of God's grace.

To rest in the eye of the storm.

PLAIN LESSON FOR LIFE

Broken: Useless or Priceless?

I stood for countless hours in our backyard gazing at the bulldozers as they slowly moved up and down a huge mound of dirt. Their big steel tracks clanked loudly as they pushed the dirt to cover trash—lots of trash. It was the Daviess County Landfill. We fully understood that it was all garbage, but that didn't stop us as curious little boys from sneaking up there on a Saturday afternoon. We would rummage through the piles hoping to find something valuable, possibly a misplaced treasure.

Periodically there would be a victory shout of some amazing find, but with some thorough examination we normally found it had some sort of defect, hence its final resting place in a landfill.

That's the human way. If its broken, it's useless.

But I'm a sentimental person. Once, I received a coffee cup as a gift and it quickly became my favorite cup—my cup of choice for enjoying my morning coffee. One morning while still half asleep, I fumbled and dropped my mug while removing it from the cupboard. In a split second, it lay shattered on the floor at my feet.

Disgusted with myself, I grabbed the broom and dust pan, swept up the mess, and tossed it into the trash. Less than thirty seconds earlier, this very cup was a best friend, one that I started every day with. Now, it was in the trash ready for the truck to come and pick it up to deliver it to the county dump.

What brought about this sudden change? The answer—brokenness. Living in a fallen world, when something is broken, it is immediately useless. That's a common mindset we carry.

So, what happens when we experience or feel broken ourselves? The truth is, we are all broken and we experience it in different ways and times. Through our own poor choices (then the reaping and sowing principle).

When we suffer the consequences of someone else's bad choices—abuses of all kinds. And then environment—diseases, accidents, or acts of nature that we have no control over.

The truth is that while something that is broken is useless to us, a broken soul is never useless to God. As a matter of fact, He is drawn to brokenness because He is a Redeemer at heart! He finds pleasure in taking those that are broken and making them new.

Jesus told the crowds, "Those who are well have no need of a physician, but those who are sick do. Go and learn what this means: 'I desire mercy, and not sacrifice.' For I came not to call the righteous, but sinners" (Matthew 9:12-13 ESV).

Points to ponder:

- Jesus is not surprised about your brokenness
- Satan wants us to believe that our brokenness renders us useless to God

- Perhaps you and I are never closer to our Creator than in our moment of deepest brokenness
- God's desire for our brokenness is redemption followed by ministry to others through compassion

"The Spirit of the Lord God is upon me; because the Lord hath anointed me to preach good tidings unto the meek; he hath sent me to bind up the brokenhearted, to proclaim liberty to the captives, and the opening of the prison to them that are bound; To proclaim the acceptable year of the Lord, and the day of vengeance of our God; to comfort all that mourn; To appoint unto them that mourn in Zion, to give unto them beauty for ashes, the oil of joy for mourning, the garment of praise for the spirit of heaviness; that they might be called trees of righteousness, the planting of the Lord, that he might be glorified. And they shall build the old wastes, they shall raise up the former desolations, and they shall repair the waste cities, the desolations of many generations" (Isa 61:1-4).

Chapter Twenty-Seven

FRESH WIND IN THE SAILS

After recovering my strength from losing my wife as well as the need to smoke cigarettes, I felt as if God's power had given me a second wind.

Therapeutically, I kept writing and singing songs, sharing my story as God gave me the opportunity. I shared with church groups, youth groups, prisoners, people at outdoor events, family gatherings, and even with a few folks in passenger vehicles while going down the road.

It was like applying healing balm to my soul every time I shared the reality of what happened, then followed it up with the testimony of God's redemption in my life.

Since music had always been a big part of me, I started entertaining the idea of making an album. I had no concept of where to start, but a few phone calls helped point me in the right direction.

I met with Nelson Miller and Maynard Mast in Nappanee, Indiana. Nelson owned a recording studio, and Maynard was an amazing musician. When I showed them the songs I had written, they offered ideas and we started preparing them for the big recording day. The songs I had written in my living room and always played with only my acoustic guitar now came to life with an assortment of instruments and talented musicians.

I was spellbound!

It took a lot of work, but a few months later I held my very own CD in my hand. I couldn't believe it! I played it all the way home from the studio and repeatedly when I got in the house.

I titled it Hero for Jesus.

Nelson had insisted that I order 1,000 CDs for the first time around. One thousand CDs! Who would ever buy them? I'd wanted to order 100 or maybe 250 to be safe. I didn't want all those disks laying around in my basement for the next twenty years. Against my better judgment, Nelson got his way, and the next thing I knew, I had 1,000 CDs along with 500 cassettes!

During that time and when I was able, I also sang with a group called Gospel Melody, a bluegrass gospel group made up of David Miller, Marion Miller, Willard Miller, and Irvin Eby.

It was a weekend in August when we were headed to Lancaster County, Pennsylvania, for an outdoor music festival.

I'd also been asked to share my story on Sunday morning. My friend Menno Miller and I drove separately, and I took most of the CDs along. That weekend, I sold every single CD I had! I also went home with more orders than the rest of my stock could fill.

I couldn't believe it. I had to order another 1,000 copies.

That recording has continued to sell over the years. Although I'm sure my voice and music skills have improved since then, people still buy that first recording. I think it's because the songs are real and emotes the power of God's love and grace to heal, forgive, and transform.

We serve an awesome Redeemer!

The album seemed to be a turning point in my progression toward healing. Although painful, I began to see how God uses our trials and brokenness to reach out and bless others. I also began to understand that we find fulfillment when we allow Him to do that.

Nobody voluntarily chooses brokenness. Given the choice, I would have most likely ran from all of the heartache, loss, and shattered dreams. But I never could have imagined what my Heavenly Father had in store.

He never wastes anything, but desires to carefully gather all the delicate pieces with one goal in mind—to turn brokenness into beauty.

HEY, SWEETS, IT'S ME

Hey Sweets, it's me. How you doing? Good.
Well, I'm doing alright. I, kinda wish you were here by my side
Hey, remember how we used to talk about Heaven and wonder
how it would be?
You do? What did you think when you were, first able to see?
Really? Well I'll bet you were happy, and really flying.
I was happy for you but, at the time I, I was, I was crying.
I just couldn't believe my little angel was really gone.
I just wanted to go with you, not left here all alone

1st Chorus
I know you're waiting and praying, and cheering for me
Knowing I wouldn't fall, if I could I see
The beauty of Heaven and the bright golden crown
When I get there I'll know, why I didn't let you down

Hey Sweets, remember that night we, prayed in my ole truck?

Yeah, Satan was really laughing, we didn't think we'd have\much luck.
And there we sat broken hearted but, God heard our cry.
And now that makes it easier, for me not to ask why.
But, remember the day you were baptized and our wedding plans from
there?
And the day we got our marriage license, people could smell
the love in the air
And the wedding Day was just right, and then came our honey moon.
But as we left your parents' house, I didn't know I'd see them again
so soon.
Remember just before the crash I was singing, How can I help you to
say Goodbye
Then just a few days later while making funeral plans, I, I just couldn't
help but cry

2nd Chorus
I can see your sweet face shining like a star,
There's not much that I know, but I know where you are
I can't wait to see the angels and hear the trumpet sound
Praise the Lord for salvation, I won't let you down
Praise the Lord for salvation. Hey Sweets, I won't let you down

—Amos Raber Jr.

ANCHORED IN JESUS

While sailing on this sea on the sea of life
When the wind of trouble blows I often wonder why
But He walked on the water and He calmed the mighty wind down
Through the power of my Jesus Hallelujah Satan's bound

—Amos Raber Jr.

Chorus

I'm anchored in Jesus while the storm rages on

The dark waves are rolling high He holds me as His own

Through His great Love there's still a song to sing

If it weren't for my Jesus, I'd fall for anything

With Jesus as your Captain the Captain of you boat

No matter how the waters roll you'll always stay afloat

Through trials and tribulations, he'll try to bring you down

Through my resurrected Jesus Hallelujah Satan's bound

—Amos Raber Jr.

After all of the heartache and grief, I felt I had finally made it through the darkest and roughest seas into the sunlight of a crystal blue future.

There was a fresh wind in my sails, and only God knew where it would take me.

Chapter Twenty-Eight

IT STARTED AT THE STOP SIGN

Several months had gone by since Amanda's funeral, and my life had begun to develop a new normal. The invitations kept coming in and many of my weekends were spent traveling to other communities sharing my story and playing music.

During the week, I spent my time at the feed mill driving trucks and heaving bagged feed. My album Hero for Jesus was doing exceptionally well in sales, and I was writing new songs and preparing for another recording date in the near future.

Gospel Melody and I were doing a concert in Paradise Pennsylvania. And since there were other music groups involved, we made some new friends. One of those had a friend back in Indiana from the same community where I lived.

On my arrival back home, connections were made and I met Becky. It didn't take long and we became close, almost like siblings. We spent time going on walks, shopping, dining, and occasionally she would invite me to join her for their family dinner events.

The rumors started flowing through the community that we were an item.

"Amos has a girlfriend," was the buzz.

But it wasn't true—not in the least bit. We were simply good pals and nothing more.

Becky included me in her circle of friends, and I soon had several new guys to hang out with. Jay was among them. We were both truck drivers and because of it, conversation came easy for us.

As a trucker at the feed mill, I did a lot of driving through the local community. I especially enjoyed the early morning deliveries. One morning as I was leaving for an early delivery, I was sipping coffee and listening to a sermon on the radio. Approaching a four-way stop sign, I slowed and stopped.

Coming from the opposite direction was a pewter Dodge Avenger. We met each other in the middle of the intersection and for no particular reason, I turned to look at the driver as we passed. She didn't see the guy in the feed truck, but I sure noticed her!

She sat in a reclined position slouched down across the car seat. Evidently, her foot was perched on the seat because her knee blocked part of the driver's side window. I had about ten seconds to look at her beautiful face, blond hair, and orange dress.

Although she seemed like she would've rather been sleeping, she sure looked lovely to me.

Who was that?

Oh, yes, I noticed her but since I knew nothing about her, I soon released her and went on with my route. A few weeks later, the exact same thing happened. I met that car at the same four-way stop as I had before.

Okay, this is a little strange.

Again, not quite as quickly as before, but a few hours later she was a misplaced memory. Especially since I had no intention of ever getting remarried. I could never imagine being able to actually love again.

†††

Becky and I continued to spend time together as close friends do. She told me the story about a close friend named Margaret. The year before, Margaret had gone to a Bible School in Georgia and met a young man named Gideon who was from South Carolina. As it so often happens at those places, the two felt a connection and when Margaret got home, she waited for his call to speak with her father.

It was all butterflies and unicorns as they began their relationship. Daily emails were anticipated, and the mailbox was excitedly checked as they continued to learn about each other. Weekend phone calls were special because they both had free minutes to use.

They planned for once-a-month visits to get to know each other's families and friends, and to spend actual face time together. The young couple and their families were enthusiastic about this new relationship, and it was obvious that they were serious about their future.

Gideon lived on a farm, but had a special love for flying and had even acquired his pilot's license. He went flying every chance he got.

There was a family in the community that was planning to move to Pennsylvania the following week. Their son, Jerry, and Gideon were in the same youth group, and Jerry wanted a plane ride before moving. And it was Gideon's delight to give him that gift.

It was a Friday afternoon when Gideon wrapped up his jobs of the day, grabbed a few things, and waved to his dad as he drove away to the plane hanger.

As he always did, Gideon walked around the plane doing his routine inspection before firing up the engine and preparing for the flight. Jerry arrived and soon the two of them were seated, strapped in and ready for departure.

The engine roared as they sped down the runway. Inside the small plane, Gideon and his friend grinned at each other with a rush of elation as they approached the end of the runway.

With the wheels lifting off the ground, they soared into the sky. No doubt, they chatted as Gideon pointed out the different farms on the patchwork below them including their family farm and other landmarks he had come to recognize from the air.

Their flight was as thrilling as the idea had promised. It just didn't get any better than that kind of freedom. Two guys, one tiny cockpit, and a universe of blue. So much space... so much distance between the earth and the sky.

Just a glimpse of an angel's view.

No one knows exactly how it happened—but that small plane fell so rapidly, crashing in a neighbor's cotton field. A mechanical error, the plane came down.

The sound of the impact, the smell of burning gasoline, the smoke that billowed for miles. Two young men were lost in their prime.

The news of the tragedy spread quickly throughout the community. Jerry was pronounced dead at the scene, but Gideon was still hanging on. His mother got to hold him for a few minutes before the paramedics rushed him off to the hospital.

The family knew someone had to make the dreaded phone call to Margaret.

Gideon's sister Karla made that call.

At her home in Milford, Indiana, it was a normal Friday for Margaret and her family. She and her mother were working around the house doing daily chores—cleaning and enjoying casual conversation—when they were interrupted.

"Gideon has been in an accident. His plane went down, Margaret. He's hurt bad," Karla told her.

Margaret and her parents quickly packed and left on the thirteen-hour journey to Olar, South Carolina. They had only driven a half mile when they got the message that Gideon had passed away en route to the hospital.

† † †

Unbelievably sad, I thought as Becky finished the story about her friend's loss. I had never met Margaret, but my heart broke for her, and I found myself wanting to find her and give her a big hug.

My mind kept wandering. *This is what it would have been like if I had let Amanda drive that day and I had been the one killed in that accident.*

I was glad for her sake that God allowed me to be the one that stayed here to face the unimaginable grief. But on the other hand, I wished so desperately I could have crossed that river to Heaven with her.

It just seemed like the best thing would have been for us to have made that trip together.

Yes, it would be a blessing to meet Margaret sometime since we had such a painful common history. Perhaps we could be a source of encouragement for each other. I certainly wasn't interested in developing anything more than that.

Since Amanda's death, the thought of getting remarried or anything close to it was unconscionable. I was positive that I could never love again. How could I? Amanda meant the world to me. The idea of giving myself to someone else seemed impossible.

I would never want to betray our love or our holy union.

When all the signs tell love to stop, can it ever find the will to start again...

...even at a stop sign?

Chapter Twenty-Nine

MYSTERY GIRL

I hated shopping, but there was a dollar store in my little town of Wakarusa, and frequently on the way home from work, I'd stop to get some groceries.

As I rounded the corner of the main aisle, there was Jay, my trucking buddy. We talked for a minute when suddenly a shopping cart intentionally bumped into Jay's.

We both looked up and I was abruptly dumbfounded!

It was the girl from the little pewter car! The one I had seen at the four-way stop—on two different occasions!

While I was reeling with surprise and confusion, it became obvious that Jay knew this young lady. They exchanged a few words, said goodbye, and she went on her way pushing her cart down the adjacent aisle.

I couldn't believe it. The Stop Sign Girl and I had a mutual friend! As strange as this encounter was, given my attitude and broken heart that still longed for my deceased wife, I quickly buried this chance encounter along with the other strange coincidental sightings.

Still... so weird.

A few weeks passed by and our group, Gospel Melody, was invited to sing at a fundraiser in Southern Indiana. We made the five-hour drive and prepared for the evening. During the concert as we sang and shared testimonies, it became official—I was now totally confused.

The Stop Sign Girl a.k.a. the Dollar Store Girl was sitting in the audience. Too strange! The community we were singing in happened to be my home community.

What in the world was she doing there? Who was this intersection woman, and how did she know my friend Jay? But there she was, in my home community. With all of the queries swirling in my head, I couldn't come up with one logical answer.

My curiosity continued to linger like smoke on a windless day. After the concert was over, I realized she had disappeared as mysteriously as she had appeared. Not a word was exchanged between us. She was gone, again.

The conundrum continued.

† † †

Life kept me busy. I spent week days working at the feed mill in anticipation of the weekends when I loaded up my guitar and CDs in the back of my Tahoe, and traveled to different communities to share my testimony of redemption.

And I loved it!

I told the painful story of losing Amanda, but also about the healing grace of God! During those times, I spent days designated to fasting and praying for God's will in my life. This was a season of healing in more than one way. God was setting me free from habits and strongholds of the past while teaching me what it meant to walk in victory.

Since I had just moved to the area, my social life consisted of my church family, my friend Becky, and some of her social circle. So, when I had the chance, I would spend an evening at church or at a friend's house. But the vast majority of time, I was at home reading scripture and talking to my Heavenly Father.

It was bittersweet. I knew I was growing and deepening my spiritual roots, but I was also keenly aware that my growth was based on the platform of the tragedy that had swept through my life.

And I was lonely.

Thank goodness for Becky. She was always inviting me out to socialize. And the music event at Dave's house on one particular Friday night was no different.

"I'm bringing my friend Margaret that I was telling you about," she added. "I'm excited that the two of you finally get to meet."

Though I was hesitant, I tried to sound positive.

"I'll be there," I said... in body anyway. I couldn't vouch for my spirit. It was still with my absent wife.

That afternoon was filled with mixed emotions. I wanted to meet Margaret, but there was something about the situation that made me uneasy. I wasn't ready in the least bit to deal with any kind of romantic feelings, and I just didn't want to get anyone's hopes up.

I guessed it wouldn't hurt to just go and put on a brave face for a friend, no matter how awkward it might be.

I met the rest of the Gospel Melody band members at Dave's early that night to rehearse some songs before people started arriving. There was a good amount of locals there, but as I glanced around the room, Becky (and friend) hadn't shown up.

After several songs, I saw the door open and in walked Becky and several other young ladies—some that I recognized and others I didn't.

But one definitely stood out to me.

Not again!

What was The Stop Sign Girl doing there?! Was she stalking me or was God playing some kind of crazy game?

At this point, nothing surprised me about her. If there was one thing I knew about this mystery gal, it was that she showed up randomly at places where I would least expect her.

Chalk up just one more random sighting.

† † †

When the concert was over, I made my way to the back of the crowd to find Becky. She said a quick "hi" but was busy visiting with some other people. The crowd cleared out briskly, and soon there was only a dozen or so people left—Becky and her friends, including the mystery girl.

"Amos," Becky called out, "Margaret is right over there. I'll introduce you to her in a minute."

I looked in the direction she was pointing and my eyes landed on you know who.

No... no way... that couldn't possibly be her...

I need some fresh air.

I spun on my heel and jetted outside. After several minutes of deep breathing, I decided to buck up and meet this enigma head-on.

I slipped back into the building only to find Becky still in her conversation.

Okay, I'm a big boy, I'll go meet her myself.

I walked over to where she was standing, stuck out my hand, and even surprised myself with the level of assertion in my voice.

"Hi, my name is Amos, and you must be Margaret."

"Hi. Yes, I'm Margaret," she answered.

Her bright smile and sparkling eyes took me off guard. She was kind and pretty. Almost effortlessly our conversation took off, and before we knew it, we had talked for an hour.

Don't say it... don't even think it.

We said our goodbyes and went our separate ways. I drove home in a daze.

I like this girl.

Her personality was contagious. But no, I couldn't be interested in starting another relationship. I wasn't ready for that.

A few weeks went by and the thought of Margaret haunted me. Yes, I had prayed about her after our first meeting, but now I felt the urgency to get more serious in prayer about her and what our meeting was all about.

Occasionally, Becky invited me to hang out with her friends, and often that included Margaret. I was attracted to her bubbly personality, her thoughtfulness, and bright smile, not to mention her golden hair and brilliant blue eyes.

I committed to a routine of fasting and praying seeking God's wisdom on how to process our new friendship. I wanted to be careful that I wasn't being drawn away into something that would cause me to violate His will for my life.

Weeks turned into months, and I became more open to the idea that our friendship could grow into a serious relationship, possibly even marriage.

Just the thought drove me back to prayer!

Six month later and in the midst of all my reservations, there was one thing I couldn't deny: I was falling in love with Margaret. What's worse, she knew nothing about it.

I found myself limiting the amount of time I spent within her circle of friends; I didn't want to run ahead of God, and I especially didn't want

Margaret to sense anything out of the ordinary. Becky and I continued to spend time together as always, talking about almost anything. But eventually we ended up discussing Margaret.

Becky, like any red-blooded female, adored the possibility of a love connection. But I made her vow to not breathe a word about my interest. I was seriously praying about it but wasn't anywhere close to being comfortable with Margaret knowing about any of it.

In spite of my reasons for trying to quell my feelings for her, it seemed like it was happening anyway.

Like a rosebud must open slowly in due season to eventually display its full brilliance, so our relationship had to develop and bloom in perfect timing—God's timing.

My intentions would remain a mystery to my Mystery Girl.

Chapter Thirty

IT'S ALL ON TAPE

It had been eight months since Margaret and I had officially met. As usual, I came home from the mill and started my evening prayer about the situation. No way was I going to run ahead of God on this.

I was enjoying taking the time to get to know her better on a casual basis, but to this point, I hadn't felt the Holy Spirit prodding to make my thoughts known to her. It seemed like a delicate balance, and I wanted to be careful. I definitely didn't want to blow this.

As I prayed about it one night, I suddenly sensed a peace that the time had come for me to move forward.

"Lord, what is the next step?" I just wasn't sure.

The praying for wisdom continued another day before I called Becky to let her know that I was okay with Margaret... knowing. She had my blessing to cough up the goods if the opportunity came.

Suddenly, I felt extremely vulnerable and questioned my decision—repeatedly—but always felt peace.

God's calling card.

I was positive about my feelings for Margaret, but there was one thing I wanted to do first. The one-year anniversary of Amanda's passing was approaching, and I wanted a special and proper closure to our life together—before I began a new chapter with anyone.

The date was January 4th, exactly one year from her funeral, and two years from our first date. Along with some friends from Fairview, we planned a special service at the little church where so many of our memories were made. And I had written a song to share that evening in honor of Amanda.

OUR FIRST ANNIVERSARY

The Snowflakes are falling so quietly to the ground
A cool December day, I'm kinda feeling down
Today's our anniversary it's only been one year
I just can't help but wonder what we'd do if you'd be here

1st Chorus
Would we go climb the Rockies together just you and I
Or lay beneath the stars of the big Montana sky?
Would we go to Texas or see the shining sea
Or would we just stay at home, all alone just you and me

Would there be a miracle perched up in her high chair
Looking like her mother with flowing blonde hair
Mommy's blue eyed angel and daddy's little girl
Making him the proudest man in all the whole world

2nd Chorus
Would we be driving down a long winding Interstate?

Watching the western sky as the sun closes the day
Would mommy be driving the car, the angel in daddy's lap
Singing Jesus Loves Me as she slips into her nap

3rd Chorus
Are you walking through a garden with a twinkle in your eye
Listening to the angels with Jesus by your side
Today's our anniversary it's only been one year
I just can't help but wonder what we'd do if you'd be here

Repeat 1st Chorus
Would we go climb the Rockies together just you and I
Or lay beneath the stars of the big Montana sky?
Would we go to Texas or see the shining the sea?
Or would we just stay at home, all alone just you and me

—Amos Raber Jr.

It was a special but difficult evening for me. Also for all the people within that little congregation that had so freely loved us. Our hearts all cried together as we reminisced about Amanda's life and the exceptional person she was to all of us in so many different ways.

As support, Becky and Margaret came for the service that evening. That night as the two of them were driving home, they discussed Margaret's future.

"When do you think you'll be ready to date again?" asked Becky.

"I'm not sure," Margaret said. "With my situation, I'm don't know if anyone would even want to date me."

"You might be surprised," Becky replied with a slight grin.

Margaret looked at her sharply. "Do you know something I don't?"

Becky kept her eyes on the road trying to maintain a straight face.

"Becky!" Margaret exclaimed.

Becky's expression took on a serious look as she turned toward Margaret. "Yes...?"

"I don't even want to know who it is," Margaret responded.

"That's okay," Becky replied. "He's serious about this and only wants God's perfect will, no matter what."

They drove home with little more to say. After a while, Margaret finally chimed in.

"Okay, I want to know. Who is it? Actually, I don't want to know. Yes, I do. Tell me...no, wait. Okay, just tell me."

"Okay, it's Amos." Becky said softly.

"What?" exclaimed Margaret. "How long have you known?"

"About eight months," said Becky.

"You mean he's been interested in me almost the whole time we've all been hanging out?" she asked slowly, as if pondering an unimaginable thought.

"Yup," replied Becky. "He wanted to get better acquainted with you while he continued praying for God's timing and, he didn't want to rush you."

Well, it didn't take long for Becky to tell me all about her conversation with Margaret. Thank goodness I didn't have long to wait through that period of tormenting inner-persecution. How would she react the next time she saw me and how awkward would it be?

Margaret's circle of friends was having a get together and I was invited. Much to my relief, I mingled with everyone easily, and things seemed relatively normal.

†††

Even though Margaret was now aware of my interest in her, I hadn't officially asked her on a date, and she hadn't given any indication if she was even remotely interested in me.

After a few weeks, which seemed like an eternity, Becky called and said Margaret was willing to meet with me to talk. I was as nervous as could be as I drove to downtown Wakarusa to meet her. When she parked her car and climbed into my Tahoe, everything was much like the first night we met—conversation came easy and we enjoyed each other's company.

The next step was the scariest of all.

Regardless of what I was used to doing when it came to dating girls, I knew that if I wanted to see Margaret again, I would need to ask her dad for his permission. No matter how I felt about Margaret, I was determined not to pursue a relationship with her without her father's blessing.

After completing my premeditated yet poorly delivered speech, he kindly invited me to their home for Sunday lunch.

† † †

The day of Margaret's birthday, Sunday, January 18th, I walked into her church.

So much was riding on this one meeting.

There she was, waiting right inside. She was absolutely stunning in a floor-length burgundy dress accented by her blonde hair. She immediately started walking toward me.

"Hey you," she smiled. "I want you to meet my dad."

I followed her across the church foyer where she approached a man in his mid-forty's. She gently placed her arm around his back, and introduced us to each other. We shook hands.

It felt great.

The day went wonderful—meeting her parents, her siblings, and having lunch around their family table was certainly a treat. After lunch, I got the chance to visit with Margaret's dad, one on one. And when I asked for his consent to see his daughter, he gave it.

The pressure was off—sort of.

Margaret and I planned our first date for Friday, January 23rd. I knocked on the door at 6:30pm with a single rose in my hand. I'm sure my face was probably as red as the flower as I waited for her to answer.

Suddenly, there she was, dressed in a long black skirt and dusty blue sweater that matched her eyes. She was hot! And I mean literally as well as figuratively. Margaret told me later the sweater made her uncomfortably warm, but she liked it so much that it didn't matter.

She graciously greeted me, and I escorted her to my Tahoe. We headed to the Boathouse Restaurant in Warsaw, Indiana, situated right on the edge of Winona Lake. The stars twinkled on the glassy water. The night was perfect. I have no idea what we ate, but our conversation flowed effortlessly as we talked about a myriad of topics: our occupations, mission work, and even marriage.

Time stood still, or at least that old cliché makes total sense now. It felt like it to us. But we realized it hadn't when we finally paused a second, took a breath, and looked at the clock.

The employees waved goodbye and then locked the door behind us as we left. We had just spent three hours at the restaurant and closed the place down!

Our first date

†††

We thoroughly enjoyed the following months as our relationship grew. Our first extended time apart was during a vacation her family took. I've never sent or received so many text messages and phone calls in my life. One call lasted for four hours!

Soon after, I left for a few weeks for a ministry tour that included some prison work, and again, it seemed that another classic cliché was true—absence makes the heart grow fonder.

I was still being invited to churches to share the story of the accident and Amanda's death, and had a backlog of dates to fill. Margaret joined me on some of those weekend trips where we would minister and then normally stay at a friend's house for the night.

The testimony part of the services became less about the accident with Amanda, and more about God's redemption in my personal life.

Although Margaret could sing wonderfully and our voices blended nicely, public singing wasn't something she had ever aspired to do. But taking baby steps, she slowly started helping me on a few songs in each service and found her groove.

And it was amazing!

It was undeniable—I loved this girl.

I loved her for many reasons, especially her fiery yet kind personality. But there was one obvious obstacle.

Our cultural differences.

I grew up in an Amish community and some variance of Amish was all I was used to. Even in our dating, this showed up in a myriad of ways. And though Amish applications will vary from one community to another, one could always find more similarities than real differences. But this was totally different.

Margaret had no Amish background at all. We found subtle contrasts irrelevant to the life we wanted to build, but there were other places where our cultural upbringing and thinking seemed to be polar opposites.

Yes, it presented some struggles. But we chose to compromise for the good of our relationship and continue the path forward.

During this time, we were committed to praying with and for each other. In my private prayers, I was seeking God's will and blessing for marriage. And just like when God gave me the green light to ask her for courtship, there it was—a release and freedom in my spirit to ask for her hand in matrimony.

Like before, I was led to seek our parents for their blessing, and they were delighted to give it.

A few months later, there was a ministry event scheduled in another community where we had some very good friends. Soon the time arrived for us to make the trip to Ohio.

For Margaret, it was just another weekend trip for three services. We were leaving on Friday evening and would likely return home late Sunday night in time for a few hours of sleep before heading off to work on Monday morning.

Not so for me. I approached this particular excursion with nerves similar to a skydiver's first jump.

I tried to act as normal as possible, but how was I supposed to do that?

What if she freaks out and says no? Well, I would know soon enough.

After telling our friends what I had planned, I ordered a dozen roses, bought the engagement gift—a specific clock I knew she wanted—and a camcorder was strategically placed to capture it all, no matter what the outcome.

When that significant Saturday morning came, our hosting friends and I drank coffee as the sun rose. But not Margaret. She was convinced there was no real oxygen to breathe that early in the AM, and could've slept till noon.

Good thing! It gave us plenty of time to rehearse the ingenious plot.

Then the moment arrived. I took a deep breath, grabbed the roses, and slowly, quietly, made my way up the stairs hoping she wouldn't randomly come out of her room and spoil it all.

I tiptoed down the carpeted aisle with the camera man right behind me as I approached her bedroom door.

I gently knocked...

"Good morning, Margaret"

I heard her stir. "I'll be down in a minute" she said sleepily.

"Uh, Honey... can you open the door now? I have something really important I need to talk to you about."

I heard the bed creak, followed by footsteps. Turning to the camera man, I smiled nervously. Getting down on one knee, I was looking up at her as she opened the door a crack, rubbing her eyes as she tried to focus on the scene before her.

"Margaret Diane Rodes, will you marry me?" I blurted out.

To my surprise and delight, she flung the door open in tears and shouted out, "Yes, I will marry you!"

Scrambling to my feet, we hugged in celebration. By this point, I had lost track of the camera man, but I think he survived it all...

cuz we got it all on tape!

Chapter Thirty-One

I DO

Instead of tired and fighting sleep, the ride home from Ohio was filled with endless chatter as we planned the big day. We had been dating for almost a year, and now we were getting married!

Monday morning came, and I was back at work like normal, but with an extra spring in my step. We began discussing all the details from start to finish: the food, flowers, wedding songs, and who the bridal party would be.

Becky would be the maid of honor, and Jeff would be the best man. Jeff had been the best man when Amanda and I got married, and Margaret asked Gideon's sister, Karla, to be one of the bridesmaids.

Invitations were made and sent out—nearly four hundred of them!

Amidst all the ceremony arranging, life went on as usual—the feed mill for me and a secretarial position for Margaret. With the wedding looming large in February, it was now December and bad weather was setting in. That always presented multiple challenges in my trucking work—getting into all the tight places was difficult when the roads were good. But the ice and snow compounded the problem.

A lot of the feed I delivered was in bulk, however, frequently the customer would request bagged feed, as well. On one particularly rainy day, temperatures hung around the freezing mark. I was preparing to deliver a load and noticed the paperwork said bagged feed, too. I grabbed the invoice and threw two fifty-pound sacks over my shoulder.

When I opened the door and took two steps down on the concrete stairs, suddenly my feet came out from under me. I had stepped onto a patch of ice.

With a hundred pounds of feed on my shoulder, I went down in a heap. I had fallen backwards and my right foot got caught under me, catching the falling weight in an unnatural position.

I felt a searing pain and heard a pop.

The mill secretary, Judy, saw it all happen and rushed out to help me up.

This was not good. My wedding was in two months!

Settling into a resting position, I called Margaret.

"Honey, I think I broke my leg. Can you go to my house, get my Tahoe, and come take me to the hospital?"

Please, tell me this isn't happening!

† † †

"Amos Raber Jr, how are you going to walk down the aisle in two months with a broken leg?"

Margaret fussed as we drove to the emergency room. I didn't know the answer to that, but I believed that God was still able to work miracles.

We arrived at the hospital where it was confirmed that my ankle was indeed broken and needed surgery as soon as possible. That was no picnic. After the surgery, the doctor gave me the approximate time I should be off the crutches and walking with a boot, but it was about week too late for our wedding.

Come on, God... do Your thing!

A few days at home under bedrest and restricted movement, I began to pray in earnest that God would miraculously heal me. And I believed He could and would!

I read the Bible stories where Jesus looked at the lame and simply said, "Arise and walk!" And I knew that it could happen. In another scripture, Jesus even said that if you have faith the size of a mustard seed, you could move a mountain. It was clear to me that when Jesus healed people, many others believed in His name because of it.

So that was it—I continued to pray.

"Lord, say the word and I will put both feet on the floor and walk. Just think of all the people that will hear the story and likely believe that You are God! The people at the hospital, the nurses and doctors. Not to mention all my friends, acquaintances... A story like this would sweep the Amish and Mennonite communities in a matter of days. Here I am, Lord. Just say the word and I will walk."

As I sat there waiting, legs dangling over the side of the bed, a still small voice began to minster to my heart.

"Amos, you are exactly right. The doctors, the nurses, family, and community would be amazed. But that's not why I allowed this to happen. I allowed it because I want to you to sit at my feet and learn a few things I want to teach you. I want to get to your heart."

I sat there, dumbfounded.

Yes, God was interested in the multitudes, but right now, His greater interest was to draw me to Himself.

Wow!

I then committed myself to using that time to deepen my spiritual life with Jesus Christ.

†††

The weeks went by and it was time for a checkup.

The doctor was pleased with the progress, and knowing our wedding date, he told me that with my present improvement, I would likely be able to walk down the aisle in a loosely tied shoe.

What a relief! And one more, small miracle in my eyes.

When that long awaited morning came, it was a beautiful day in February. I had got my Tahoe detailed and it sat outside the church door glistening in the sun.

The day was as bright and cheerful as the mood in the air, although I was bit limited in what I could do with a recovering broken ankle. Becky arrived with the order of roses. I had planned a progression of giving roses to Margaret—one on our first date; a dozen when we got engaged, and eighteen on the wedding day.

†††

There wasn't anything traditional or spiritual about my fragrant endeavor, just a unique little something to show her how much I adored her. And, if we ever had children, I would give her two dozen roses to celebrate her entering motherhood.

Soon, the place was buzzing with activity. The wedding coordinator was doing her job—everything from food preparation and pictures to table set-up. After the many weeks of planning, all the pieces to this giant puzzle were all fitting together.

The guests were starting to arrive, and soon the wedding ceremony was underway. The pastor took his place at the front of the church and summoned us to come if it was still our desire to exchange vows.

Margaret and I held hands, promised our love and devotion—in sickness and in health—and to live out the rest of our days on earth as one in Christ.

"In the presence of God and these witnesses, I pronounce you husband and wife."

Margaret and I turned toward the gathering of our loved ones and friends.

He went on, "It is my pleasure to introduce to you for the very first time, Mr. and Mrs. Amos Raber!"

Margaret and I stepped off the platform and walked as briskly as I was able toward the back of the church, the bridal party following close behind.

Privacy... it's all we wanted at that moment. Since our very first conversation, we knew and later agreed to save our first kiss until we were married.

† † †

Margaret and I had chosen soup, sandwiches, and cheesecake for the reception. The place vibrated with conversation as family and friends from near and far chatted over their food. But the noise fell silent as someone tapped the microphone, starting the reception's open dialogue time.

It was an opportunity for anyone to share something about the bride or groom. One after another, people offered personal insight, funny stories, and heartwarming renditions of how Margaret and I seemed to fit together perfectly from the start.

After a while, when it seemed that everyone had said their peace, Margaret's mother got up and took the mic.

"I didn't share this story with Margaret and Amos until I knew they were going to be married. Now, they'd like me to share it with you.

"A little over two years ago, I'd never heard of Amos Raber. But one evening, I was reading the newspaper and I saw the obituary for a young lady who had died in an accident. I saw that her husband was Amos Raber, and I wondered who he was. When I finished reading it, a voice—not audible, but very clear—told me, 'This man will be Margaret's husband.'

"My first thought was that it wasn't proper or respectable to have thoughts like that when his wife was not buried yet. My next thought was that I didn't even know him. How could this be?

"My third thought was, 'Well Lord, I'm just going to leave it in Your hands because I sure don't know how it will be worked out.' I kind of just put it in the back of my mind, but I kept my ears open.

"A few months later, I started hearing about Amos Raber and his testimony and recordings, but I still didn't know much about him.

"Then one night after Margaret had gone with some friends to a singing with a group of people, she called home to say she would be late. She was talking to a guy who had lost his wife in an accident. Margaret could relate having lost Gideon in the plane crash just the year before.

"The next morning, I asked her who the young man was, but she said she couldn't remember his name. I asked if it was Amos Raber, and she said she thought it was.

"I thought, 'Well, she just doesn't know yet!'

"Summer came, and Margaret told me one evening, 'Mom, I keep running into Amos Raber around town. He sure is a sincere Christian.'

"Then fall came, and Margaret finally resolved some issues she had concerning the death of Gideon, and she told me she was ready to move on in her life. She just wasn't sure if she wanted to start dating, yet. About that same time, Margaret told me Amos was interested in someone, but she didn't know who. I almost asked her if it was her, but I knew not to rush God's timing.

"In January, Margaret came home one day and said, 'Mom, what kind of guy do you think I need for a husband?' I told her, first, a sincere Christian. And second, a stronger personality than you. Then she told me she had just found out Amos was interested in her. She was so surprised, she had no idea.

"A few weeks later they started dating, and I guess you know the rest of the story. It was so wonderful and inspiring to see how God worked this all out. His timing is always perfect. This is also evidence of God's planning and care for their lives before they even knew each other, and it's with joy and peace in my heart that we give Margaret into Amos's care."

We all sat marveling at the divine providence of God. Then it was my turn. I got up and went to the mic and sang a song I had written for Margaret for our wedding day.

I'LL TRY

There won't be a fancy house, that catches the human eye
You won't drive around in a long black sedan
But I'll try to do the duties of a husband and a friend
To fulfill the purpose of an upright godly man

Chorus
And I'll try to stop the bullets before they get to you
And plow spiritual ground for you to follow through
I'll try to assure you with hope and security

That you can hold on to me while I'm holding on to Him

If time brings little ones that come into our home
I pray the Lord will help us give them everything we have
And after they're grown and moved away from home
I hope that their heroes will be their own mom and dad

Bridge
'Cause we'll still be together, holding until the end
Spending our lives just being best of friends

After the song, Margaret joined me at the microphone, and we thanked all the guests for coming then said goodbye.

We were married and were leaving on our honeymoon! My Mystery Girl...

at the stop sign...

in the dollar store...

now in my arms.

I was overwhelmed with joy

After so many broken pieces and questions, it seemed like I had just witnessed my miracle of miracles. It only confirmed in my heart that though I hadn't seen Him and only rarely felt Him, there had always been a Master that was lovingly moving behind the scenes. That His miracles would eventually arrive, reflecting His goodness and love.

He is so good.

He is God.

And He is a Redeemer.

I realized that I had experienced something very profound. Redemption.

Just Plain Redemption.

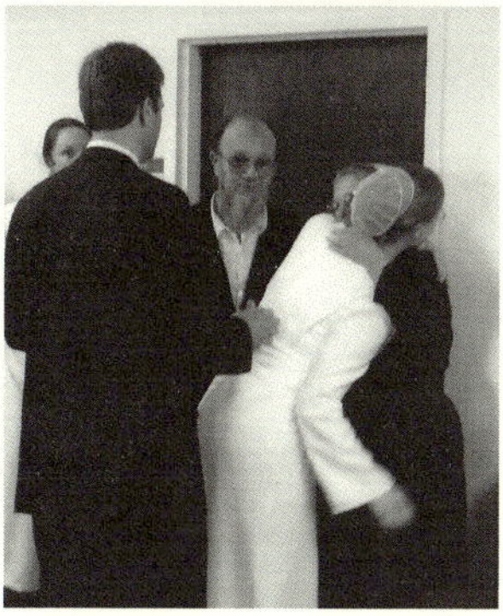

ABOUT THE AUTHOR

Amos started singing publicly when he was in his early teens and continues being involved in music and singing to this day. Amos and Margaret started singing together while they were dating and have enjoyed working with several other ministry groups along the way. They served a three year with Gospel Express Ministries from North Carolina for three years focusing primarily in Prison Ministry.

Amos and Margaret have five children and live in Northern Indiana where Amos serves on the pastoral team in their home congregation. Margaret enjoys the art of food and being a homemaker. They travel in a bus about half the year, singing and sharing in testimony, renewal meetings, Christian cruises, prison work, and wherever God opens the door.

Their ministry has now evolved into a family effort with the children taking an active part in singing and playing several different instruments. They count it a blessing and honor to use their talents in service for the Savior, and desire to bring encouragement wherever God calls them.

BYGRACE MINISTRY

PO Box 225 Ligonier, Indiana 46767

www.bygraceministry.com

Facebook: ByGrace Ministry / Amos and Margaret Raber